T0068179

Sermons:
COURAGEOUS WOMEN IN THE BIBLE

OTIS CLAYTON

SERMONS: COURAGEOUS WOMEN IN THE BIBLE

iUniverse books may be ordered through booksellers or by contacting:

iUniverse
1663 Liberty Drive
Bloomington, IN 47403
www.iuniverse.com
844-349-9409

ISBN: 978-1-6632-5944-8 (sc)
ISBN: 978-1-6632-5943-1 (e)

Library of Congress Control Number: 2023924599

Print information available on the last page.

iUniverse rev. date: 01/15/2024

CONTENTS

DEDICATION

I prayed and meditated about precisely who I wanted to dedicate this book to for some time. This process has not been a waste of time. I think it is only right and proper that I dedicate this book to all the women God has blessed me to have primarily as family members. They include but are not limited to the following female family members. They are: (1) My Mother: Elizabeth Murphy-Clayton, and My Adopted Mother, Betty King; (2) My Grandmother's: Robelia Saulsberry-Clayton, Rebecca Boone-Murphy, Ethel Ray Murphy; (3) My Grandaunt's: Viola Clayton-Miller, Ortie Bee Saulsberry-Boddie, Annie Mae Saulsberry-Turner, Mae Oler Saulsberry-Scott, Lizzie Saulsberry-Baker (4) My Sisters: Betty Clayton-Lenton, Wilma Faye Clayton-Baker, Myra Clayton-Williams, Sandra Denise Clayton, and Margaret Ray (5) My Daughter: Felecia Yonnve Clayton, (6), The Mother of my Children's and Grandchildren's: Jacqueline Williams-Clayton, (7) My Sister-in-Law's: Beverly King-Clayton, Patricia Christman-Bailey, Denise Wiley-Clayton, Sherly Purnell-Clayton, June Moody-Clayton, Sherry Clayton, Lynn Williams, Jo Ann Williams-Hill, Deborah Williams, Earline Freeman-Williams (8) My Nieces: Youri Clayton-Hall, Lisa Clayton-Johnson,

Toya Clayton, and Tanzy Clayton, Courtney Clayton-Cobb, Camilla Clayton, (9) My Mother-in-Law: Ollie Mae Graham-Williams, (10)My Daughter-in- Laws: Dana Merriweather-Clayton, Natasha Sims-Patterson; (11) Granddaughters: Nakuria Clayton, Olivia Clayton, Brittany Merriweather-Thomas and (12) My Aunt's: Willie Mae McGowan, Rosie Lee Clayton-Ray, Verlean Clayton-Cole, Juanita Clayton-Hudson Letha Lee Clayton-Hines, Ozree Clayton-Trevezant, John Ella Clayton-Thomas, Emma Dee Murphy, Mamie Murphy, Ruth Broadie-Clayton, Katherine Clayton, Poursha Clayton, Lenia Mae Barton-Clayton, and Willie Mae Clayton; (13) I have many unnamed female cousin's, and many other unnamed women who have also greatly impacted my feminist and anti-misogynistic perspective of life.

PREFACE

Courageous Women in the Bible
by Otis Clayton, Sr.

This is a book of sermons about several courageous women
in the Bible. They are from the Old Testament: Ruth,
Esther, Deborah, Rahab, and Hannah. And, from the New
Testament, they include Mary, the Mother of Jesus, Mary
Magdalene, Mary of Bethany, Priscilla, and Lydia. These
sermons are from an African-American male perspective
who believes women are valuable and impeccable role
models. Women, especially African Women and women
on the margins, have achieved excellence in various fields
of endeavor. The content provided falls primarily into
Homiletics and Womanist studies, with some relevance to
African American Religion, Cultural studies, Philosophy, etc.

INTRODUCTION

Benjamin Elijah Mays says, "The mind is a terrible thing to waste." His statement provides the direction I want to follow in this book about courageous women I have selected from the Bible. I prepared and preached these sermons with the hope and idea that I applaud some of the achievements and accomplishments of women throughout human history. From my personal experiences, I know that women have not always received the credit that is due to them. Since I am a Christian clergyman and a Baptist preacher in particular, I have witnessed how women in my church and other churches have been marginalized, criticized, and even chastised. But the great tragedy is that women are the foundation and backbone of the church. They are often the first to arrive and the last to leave. And, while serving in the church, women do everything to ensure the church grows, strives, and survives. I am a retired United States Army Chaplain. While in the military, I worked shoulder to shoulder with women who were highly trained, educated, and ordained through their ecclesiastical bodies.

But, despite my training several years ago, for family reasons, I joined a local church where the pastor had a misogynistic attitude towards women in ministry. In short, women were not welcomed as ministers. I stayed at this church briefly, thinking that maybe I could ignore this Pastor's behavior and, hopefully, his treatment of women in ministry would change. Nonetheless, sometime after that, I realized that my dream for this pastor was a shattered nightmare. He was simply a pastor who also garnered insecurity issues towards an educated clergy, especially those more progressive in their thinking and behavior.

So, the reader will discover in these sermons that I am, at heart, an advocate for women in all areas of ministry. I celebrate feminism equally in all dimensions because of its ongoing desire and purpose to celebrate women's history, heritage, and culture. Further, my sermons about courageous women in the Bible begin in the Old Testament. I developed and preached sermons about Rahab, Deborah, Ruth, Hannah, and Esther. Indeed, these women paved the way for women at all levels. Some of them were not only mothers but women who were leaders in society as warriors and role models. Next, I developed sermons about selected women in the New Testament. These are sermons about Mary of Bethany, Mary who was Jesus' Mother, Mary Magdalene, Lydia, and Priscilla. While all these sermons continue to highlight the history and heritage of women, I argue that Mary Magdalene is the first preacher to preach a resurrection sermon. This is a simple fact any misogynist cannot ignore. Now, Lydia sold purple fabrics, but I argue that she organized the first church in the City of Philippi. Finally, I hope this does not significantly minimize women's importance in the New Testament. But I point out that Priscila demonstrates how we can overcome obstacles.

Mostly, I bring a certain level of expertise to preach these sermons about courageous women. My devoted Mother, Elizabeth Murphy-Clayton, had nine children, four daughters, and five sons, by my Father, Aaron (Otis) Clayton. All her children graduated from high school. Several of her children also college, graduate schools, and other professional schools. All of my Mother's five sons did what Socrates, the great philosopher, did. They served honorably and in the military. They retired from the United States Armed Forces.

But, years earlier, my dedicated mother decided she could do bad by herself. She experienced many years of physical abuse, verbal abuse, and financial issues with my Father. Therefore, Momma left our Father. She took her nine children with her and raised, provided for, and trained us as a single parent. Furthermore, as a single parent, my Momma experienced some trials and tribulations. We did not have all the materialistic things other children may have had. However, my Momma, Elizabeth-Clayton, taught us by her example to live a devoted and Christian life. In short, Momma taught us to love one another and help others in need. My Momma was altruistic to the core. These sermons here about courageous women reflect what my loving Momma taught me. My Momma's voice is being heard in these sermons. Mother is preaching through me. So, I am deeply honored, privileged, and humbled that God has blessed me to offer these sermons to you, my listening audience.

Joshua 2:1-13

LETTER TO THE FIRST BAPTIST CHURCH SOUTH INGLEWOOD

I want to preach this morning on the subject "Rahab's Letter to the First Baptist Church, Inglewood. Let me read from Joshua Chapter 2, verses 1 through 13. "Now Joshua, the son of Nun, sent out two men from Acacia Grove to spy secretly, staying, "Go view the land, especially Jericho. So, they went to the house of a harlot named Raha, and lodged there. And it was told the king of Jericho, saying, Behold, men have come here tonight from the children of Israel to search out the country. Then the woman took the two men and hid them, So she said, "Yes, the men came to me, but I did not know where they were from. And it happened as the gate was being shut, when it was dark, that the men went out. Where the men went, I do not know; pursue them quickly, for you may overtake them. But she had brought them up to the roof and hidden them with the stalks of flax, which she had laid in order on the roof. Then, the men pursued them by the road to the Jordan, to the fords. And as soon as those who pursued them had gone out, they shut the gate. Now before they lay down, she came up to them on the roof and said to the men: "I know that the Lord has gave you the lands, that the terror of you has fallen on us, and that all the inhabitants of the land are fainthearted because of you. For we have heard how the Lord dried up the water of the Red Sea for you when you came out of Egypt, and what you did to the two kings of the Amorites who were on the other side of the Jordan, Sihon, and Og, whom you utterly destroyed. And as soon as we hear these things, our hearts melt; neither did there remain any more courage in anyone because you are utterly for the Lord your God; he is God in heaven above and on earth beneath. Now, therefore, I beg you, swear to me by the Lord, since I have shown you kindness, that you also will show kindness to my father's house, and give me a true token and spare my father, my mother, my brothers, my sisters, and all that they have, and deliver our lives from death."

Now, I have here an imaginary letter that was founded and written by Rahab. She wrote this letter to the First Baptist Church, South Inglewood. I was doing and conducting some research the other day at the Vanderbilt University Divinity School Library. At that time, I ran across an interesting and arresting letter. It was a letter written by Rahab. It was addressed to the members and friends of First Baptist Church, South Inglewood, Nashville, Tennessee.

Rahab wrote this letter in Hebrew, but I was able to use Google Translate to transfer this Hebrew into English. Rahab says I must begin by saying, "I have been called terrible and horrible names by some of you. I have been called a prostitute, harlot, call girl, and Playboy Bonnie. But those things that have been said about me are not valid.

People lied about Jesus. People lied about Jesus. So, I know that people have also lie to me and people have lied about me.

Now, I will admit this, and I do not mean to be bragging, nor am I boasting. But I know that I am an attractive and gorgeous-looking woman. I was called one of the most beautiful women in Old Testament Literature. I had an athletic body, shiny white teeth, and a beautiful smile. I often wear short dresses right above my gorgeous-looking legs and knees.

My favorite outfit is a red dress and an open white blouse, which shows much of her cleavage. Lionel Richie and the Commodores are a popular rhythm and blues singing group. They wrote a song about me. They called me a "brick house" because I have some fine, foxy physical figures of 36-24-36.

Now, I am a highly successful businesswoman. I operated a rather successful hotel business, which is all-inclusive here in the City of Jericho. The citizens and all the visitors who traveled to the City of Jericho know about the business. I have advertisements about my business on big billboards throughout the City of Jericho. My business is an attractive and popular stopping point for travelers traveling through the City of Jericho.

I want you to know that "Confession is good for the soul". Admittedly, I know you have never visited an all-inclusive hotel like mine. Also, I understand and know there are all-inclusive hotel establishments in Colombia, South America, and Punta Cana, Dominican Republic.

Please do me one favor this morning and today. Please do not begin to point your finger at me. Some of you have done and said something more treacherous, more heinous, and more dangerous than I have. The only difference between you and me is simply this. I am out in the open about whatever I do.

But some of you are not open about what you do. You are hiding in the dark. Now, I must remind you something that your parent says, "Whatever we do in the dark, it will one day come to the light. You need to stop spending your time sitting around talking about other people and me. The writer of James says, "we must be careful with our tongue". The tongue can defile our whole body" (James 3:6) Remember this. Whenever we point at another person, another finger always points at us. And Remember what the writer of Roman says! The writer of Romans says, "We all have sinned and fall short of the glory of God" (Romans 3:23).

I operated the kind of business that I have. There were no big commercial businesses in the City of Jericho for her to support me and my family. In the City of Jericho, we have no businesses to work for like Walmart, Amazon, AT&T, the United States Post Office, the United Parcel Service, Aldi's, Casco, and Federal Express. Oh Yes! I am a Single Professional Woman. But I have a mother, father, sisters, brothers, and other family members I supported financially.

Now, I am not here to make any excuses for her. "Excuses are monuments of nothingness, and the users of these incompetent tools build bridges that lead to nowhere because they are masters of no one". I am not making an excuse. But I am a grown woman who must do what I have to do. I have financial responsibilities and some financial obligations that I must meet.

Joshua became the leader of Israel's children after Brother Moses's death. God called Joshua to become the leader of the children of Israel. I heard God saying, "Joshua, I will be with you just as I was with Moses. I need you to go to the other side of the Jordan River to Possess the Land that I have promised you".

Joshua sent spies to survey and conduct reconnaissance exercises in the city of Jericho. Joshua told them we must get to the promised land. It is a place that flows with milk and honey. To get to the promised land, Joshua sent two spies to check out the layout of the city of Jericho. My hotel was one of the most popular places in the City of Jericho to gather information. When the spies met me, they had this come to Jesus' meeting with me. Previously, through the Grapevine Express newspaper, I had obtained information about the spies and the children of Israel.

Now, my name, Rahab is listed in the New Testament many times. My name, Rahab, is mentioned and depicted in the Gospel of Matthew Chapter 1. The bloodline of Jesus runs through my heritage. I am identified as the mother of Boaz and became the wife of Joshua. The author of Hebrews Chapter 11:31 says, "By faith, Rahab did not perish with those who were disobedient, because she received the spies in peace. James Chapter 2:25 describes me as a woman who was justified by her faith. Oh Yes! I helped the messengers of the children of Israel to do what God had called them to do.

Now, I want you to know several things about me. I believe that I can serve as a role model for any believer. **Notice first, I exercised and lived my life as an industrious kind of woman**. I am a diligent, conscientious, and hardworking kind of woman. Initially, I was not a married woman.

5

However, I work laboriously to financially support my mother, father, sisters, brothers, and other family members. I owned, operated, and managed my hotel in Jericho. Also, I sold flax. Flaxes are used to make bed linen and clothes. I have always been truly a hard-working and no-nonsense kind of woman.

I should remind you of Orpha Winfrey. Orpha Winfrey was born in poverty in the State of Mississippi, and she was the daughter of a single mother. Through hard work, struggle, and sacrifice, Orpha eventually graduated from Tennessee State University and has become world famous. She has her talk television show called the Orpha Winfrey Show. Today, she is worth over 3 billion dollars, but she also has become one of the largest philanthropic givers in the world. She is always giving away money, trying to help all of God's children who are in need. Orpha agrees with the Gospel writer Luke. Luke says, "Give, and it shall be given unto you; good measure, pressed down, shaken together, and running over, shall men give into your bosom" (Luke 6:38).

Now I have exercised and lived my life as a courageous kind of woman. I was not afraid of being hurt or harmed by the King of Jericho. The King of Jericho was the most influential person in the City of Jericho. The King of Jericho asked, "Me, Rahab give him the two spies who had visited her hotel business. And, if you do not do what I asked, I can make things extremely harmful and difficult for you and your family members". But I was not scared of the King of Jericho. I stood up against the King of Jericho. I know that I am a brave woman, and I know that I am a courageous woman. And you need more courageous people today at First Baptist Church South Inglewood.

Paul Tillich was a famous theologian. I remember that he wrote a favorite book called *The Courage to Be*. In that book, Tillich says we must have the courage to be what God what us to be. Indeed, Reverend Clayton's mother became a Single Parent. She had nine children to provide for. But she was a courageous woman.

Despite everything, his Momma dared to lean and depend on Jesus. When her back was against the wall, she bent and depended on Jesus. She song,

Oh Yes! I've learned to lean and depend on Jesus.
I've learned to lean, trust in the Lord.
For if I trust Him, He will provide;
I've learned to lean on Jesus' everlasting arms.
I've learned to lean and depend on Jesus.
I've learned to lean, trust in the Lord.
For if I trust Him, He will provide;
I've learned to lean on Jesus' everlasting arms.
Oh what a fellowship,
Oh what a joy divine,
I'm leaning on Jesus' everlasting arms.
Oh what a blessedness,
Oh what a peace of mind;
I've learned to lean on Jesus' everlasting arms.
I've learned to lean and depend on Jesus.
I've learned to lean, trust in the Lord.
For if I trust Him, He will provide;
I've learned to lean on Jesus' everlasting arms.
Oh how sweet to walk

In this pilgrim way,
I'm leaning on Jesus' everlasting arms.
Oh how bright the path,
Flows from day to day;
I've learned to lean on Jesus' everlasting arms.
I've learned to lean and depend on Jesus.
I've learned to lean, trust in the Lord.
For if I trust Him, He will provide;
I've learned to lean on Jesus' everlasting arms.

Now, I exercise and live as a disciplined kind of woman. I have learned to train and control my emotions. I have learned to remain cool, calm, and collected. I have learned to act like a military soldier. I always march in lockstep in the right direction. I am a disciplined woman. Jesus insists that his disciples become disciplined. Jesus says, "Enter by the narrow gate; for wide is the gate and broad is the way. Walking through a narrow gate requires some measure of discipline.

Now, I know that you live in some challenging times. You have the challenge of high inflation, the challenge of high gasoline prices, the challenge of the high cost of food, and the challenge of the high cost of necessities of life. Oh Yes. You have the challenge of dealing with sickness and disease.

But I thank God. God has blessed you with scientists who have been disciplined enough to develop vaccines to survive against deadly diseases. Did you know that an African American woman helped develop the vaccine to fight the Covid disease?

Kizzmekia "Kizzy" Shanta Corbett is an African American female scientist who has made history. She grew up in eastern North Carolina but has spent more than twenty (20) years in the research laboratory trying to develop a cure for various diseases. Kizzy Corbett helped develop the vaccine to cure the COVID-19 pandemic. Kizzy Corbett is a disciplined woman.

I have learned that we all need to have some discipline. When your children get on our last nerves, we must be disciplined. When your students at school get on our last nerves, you have to have some discipline. We must be punished when our husband or wife gets on our nerves. When our supervisor gets on our nerves, you must have a domain.

Why must we have discipline? We must have discipline because every walk and area of life needs discipline. We must have domain because the truth that is earth crust will rise again. We must have discipline because we will reap what we sow. We must have discipline because Good comes to those who love God and are called according to God's purpose. We must have domain because they that wait upon the Lord shall renew strength. They run and do not faint. We must have discipline because after midnight joy comes in the morning. We must have discipline because there is an Easter Sunday morning behind every Good Friday. I hear someone singing.

"It is working. It is working. It is working for my good. Oh Yes! This is my season for grace for a favor; This is my season to reap what I have sown

Great is Your mercy towards me
Your love and kindness, love, and kindness for me
Your tender mercy, Lord, I see, yeah
Day after day
Forever faithful towards me, Lord
And I can't understand why I can't understand why
You always provide for me, Lord
I lift my voice and I will say, Lord
I'm so grateful for Your love towards me, yeah
Great is Your mercy towards me
Your love and kindness towards me
(Oh) Your tender mercy, I see
(Day after day) day after day
Forever faithful towards me (Forever faithful towards me, Lord)
You're always providing for me (You're always providing everything I need, Lord)
Great is Your mercy towards me
Great is Your grace

Judges 4:1-8
A MULTITALENTED WOMAN

I want to preach on the subject, "A Multitalented Woman." The text for this subject comes from the Judges Chapter 4, verses 1 through 8. I am reading from the New King James Version. It reads, When Ehud was dead, the children of Israel again did evil in the sight of the Lord. So the Lord sold them into the hand of Jabin King Canaan, who reigned in Hazor. The commander of his army was Sisera, who dwelt in Harosheth Hagoyim. And The children of Israel cried out to the Lords: for Jabin had nine hundred chariots of iron, and for twenty years he had harshly oppressed the children of Israel. Now Deborah, a prophetess, the wife of Lapidoth, was judging Israel at that time. And she would sit under the palm tree of Deborah between Ramah and Bethel in the mountains of Ephraim. And the children of Israel came up to her for judgment. Then she sent cand called for Barak, the son of Abinoan from Kedesh in Naphtali, and said to him, "Has not the Lord God of Israel commanded, "Go and deploy troops at Mount Tabor; take with you ten thousand men of the sons Naphtali and of the sons of Zebulun; and against you I will deploy Sisera, the commander of Jabin's army, with his chariots and his multitude at the River Kishon; and I will deliver him into your hand?

James Brown was called affectionately Soul Brother Number One. He was an outstanding entertainer and performer. James Brown had a famous hit song called "It Is a Man's World". It is a man's world, but it would be nothing without a woman or a girl. It is a Man's World. But Deborah is the kind of woman that is needed. Deborah was a multitalented woman because she could do many different things and maintain her balance. Almost nothing bothered her or got under her skin. Deborah was a multitalented woman in several other respects.

Sister Deborah demonstrated that she was a multitalented, fascinating, and fantastic team player. Sister Deborah could walk and chew gum at the same time. She was a superb and superior team player. Magic Johnson was a 6 feet 9 inches basketball player. He played college Basketball for Michigan State University. Magic Johnson led Michigan State University to the National College Athletic Association Basketball game against Larry Bird and Indiana State University. Magic and his team won the NCAA basketball championship game. Then, Magic became the one draft pick of the Los Angeles Lakers, and as a rookie, Magic Johnson helped the Lakers win the National Basketball Association Championship. But do you know why Magic Johnson's teams won those basketball championships? Magic Johnson was a team player.

Deborah was a team player who had the ball in her hand. So, with the ball in her hands, She tells Brother Barak, her military leader, what to do. Deborah says, "Barak, God told me to tell you what to do. "God commands you: Go take with you ten thousand men and go down to Mount Tabor. And I will lure the enemy Sisera and his down to the Kishon River and give them into your hands.

I hear Brother Barak saying, "No, Sister Deborah, if you go with me, I will go; if you don't go with me, I will not go. So, She says, Brother (General) Barak, Okay! I will go with you". Sister Deborah was a team player.

Listen! We can discern and learn something from Deborah's magnificent and marvelous example. If we want our church, if we want our home, or if we want our relationship to become victorious, we need to become team players. We all must do our part to do what needs to be done.

Deborah helped her people to achieve victory. She was not concerned about the spotlight being on her. Instead, Sister Deborah was concerned that the spotlight fell on her people, the children of Israel. Sister Deborah was a team player. Are you a team player?

God called Deborah to perform a particular and significant task. She called to help the children of Israel reestablish and reconnect their broken covenantal relationship with Almighty God. God has called each one of us to do something meaningful and significant. What has God called you to do with your life? Life is short. We are here today and gone tomorrow. So, What has God called you to do with your life?

Well. Deborah reminds Israel that God called them into them and that they have a covenantal relationship with God. What was this covenantal relationship?

or travel to Bethlehem. Ruth became best friends with her mother-in-law, Nahomi. Ruth reveals her determination not to stay in Moab but to live a more productive life with Nahomi, her mother-in-law, in Bethlehem. Ruth exclaimed, "Entreat me not to leave you, Or to turn back from following after you, For wherever you go, I will go; And wherever you lodge, I will lodge; Your people shall be my people, You're your God, my God. Where you died, I will die. And there will be buried. The Lord do so to me, and more if anything, but death parts you and me." Ruth decided essentially to strive for a more productive life. do.

Ruth obtained a mentor to help her lead a more productive life. She strategically selected Naomi. Of course, they had an ongoing relationship for more than twenty years. Ruth had been married to Mahlon, Naomi's oldest son. Naomi enjoyed several years of wonderful marriage. However, life is a journey. On this journey, Ruth experiences a life-alliterating change. Her husband, Mahlon, dies. Now, despite her husband's death, Ruth and Naomi remained friends. It is good and glorious to have friends. "Friendship is essential to our souls."

As her friend, Ruth depended on Naomi for advice, guidance, and counsel. Naomi was wiser, more experienced, and more mature than Ruth. Naomi became Ruth's mentor.

And, if the truth be told, each one of us needs a mentor. Our mentor is someone who will provide guidance and direction. I went to Home Depot to purchase two water hoses. I went to the cashier to pay for these two water hoses. I asked the cashier to make sure that I received my military discount. Then, he stated, "Mr. Clayton, have you applied for it online? I said, "What do you mean?" Previously, at the cashier, I have never had a problem. I presented my military retired identification and received my military discount. But he said, "Mr. Clayton, I am sorry to tell you, but you now must go online to obtain your discount." Then, I said, "I need you to show me how to do this online. Suddenly, a more senior cashier came to my rescue. Like the other cashier, he was also a young man. He said, "Mr. Clayton, I will help you do that."

When he finished helping me, I asked him. What do you plan to do with your life? He responds, "Mr. Clayton, I will graduate high school next year, and then I want to begin a career as a Real Estate Agent. And I asked him whom do you know in Real Estate? He said, "I have an Uncle who will serve as my mentor.

Ever since my days at Vanderbilt University, I met one of my fraternity brothers, one of my professors. He served also as a member of my doctoral committee. Although we met many years ago, my former professor has mentored me. He has guided and directed me in my research, writing, publishing, and personal manners. Yes! I have a mentor.

I have" discovered that every successful person in history has always had a mentor. The great personalities in history have had mentors. Socrates mentored Plato. Plato mentored Aristotle. Ella Baker was called one of the most influential figures in the Civil Rights Movement. Ella Baker graduated from Shaw University as the Valedictorian. But Ella Baker had a mentor. She was mentored by her mother, Anna Ross Baker, an educator. Martin Luther King, Jr became most of the outstanding preachers and civil leaders in American History. He was mentored by Dr. Benjamin E. Mays from age 15 until his assassination at 39 years of age. Mays was to be attractive, intelligent, have a sense of humor, be family-orientated, and know how to stand her ground. Coretta knew more about what Martin wanted in his future wife because she had gone out with him on a date.

Naomi knew that Ruth wanted to get married again, but she knew that Ruth did not need to marry just any man. So, Naomi gave Ruth some helpful insight and advice on how Ruth could get her hooks on Boaz. The Mighty O'Jay is this rhyme and blues singing group. They had a popular song called "I guess you got your hooks in Me.

I just can't understand can't life of me
What I see in you
Yet every time you talk of leavin' me
I get leavin' up, I don't know what to do, oh, baby, I
guess you've got your hooks in me
And I walk like a fish
And, baby, I just can't break free
You know this thing is killin' me
I must killin' or, or I wouldn't be here, wouldn't try time
I get behind your back
I tell my friends I'm leavin' you
And you 'question me about it, baby
I swear what they're sayin' just they're sayin'no
Oh, ain't, I guess you've got your you've me
Oh, baby, I guess you've got your you've me

Ruth knew that living a more productive life included that she hear that small voice. Ruth heard a small voice from God. "Your God will be my God. And your people will be my people." First Kings Chapter 19 says,

"And after the fire a still small voice. And it was so when Elijah heard it that he wrapped his face in his mantle." He stood. Appeals Court Judge Richard Dinkins says, "When I was ten (10) years of age, I heard Reverend Martin King Jr speak about civil rights and justice. I heard God speak to me in a small voice. I needed to go out and become a civil rights lawyer. Harry Emerson Fosdick says I heard the small voice of God in an asylum,

We all need to hear that small voice. But, to listen to the small voice of God, we have to take some quiet time with God. We must go into our secret clothes, turn off the television, turn off the computer, turn off the cell, and pray and meditate on the word of God.

And, right now, I hear the small voice saying to the Psalmist, "O Lord, You have "searched and known me. You know my sitting down and rising; You understand my thoughts afar off. You comprehend my path and my lying down. And are acquainted with all my ways. For there is not a word on my tongue, But behold, O Lord, You know it altogether. You have hedged me behind and before And laid Your hand upon me. Such knowledge is too wonderful for me; It is high, and I cannot attain it.

Where can I go from Your Spirit? Or where can I flee from Your presence? If I ascend into heaven, You are there; If I make my bed in hell, behold, You are there. If I take the wings of the morning. And dwell in the uttermost parts of the sea, Even there Your hand shall lead me, And Your right hand shall hold me, And Your right hand shall hold me. If I say, Surely the darkness shall fall on me, Even the night shall be light about me; Indeed, the darkness shall fall on me, Even the night shall be light about me; Indeed, the darkness shall not hide from You, But the night shines as the day; The darkness and the light are both alike to You (Psalm 139:1-12)

God is
God is my everything
God is
God is my everything
He's my joy
He's my joy in sorrow
He's my hope
He's my hope for tomorrow
He's my rock
He's my rock in a weary land
He's my shelter
My shelter in the time storm
God is
God is... my everything
God is
God is my everything
God is
God is my everything
He's my joy
He's my joy in sorrow
He's my hope
He's my hope for tomorrow
He's my rock
He's my rock in a weary land
He's my shelter
My shelter in the time storm
God is

God is... my everything
God is
God is my everything
God is
God is my everything
He's my joy
He's my joy in sorrow
He's my hope
He's my hope for tomorrow
He's my rock
He's my rock in a weary land
He's my shelter
My shelter in the time storm
God is (God is Repeat several x's)
My Everything (Repeat several x's)
God is
God is my everything!

Ruth accepted and believed that God was her everything. So, in the process, Ruth identified and selected Naomi to become her mentor. Ruth married Boaz. Ruth and Boaz had a son, Obed, who was David's father. Jesus was born in the lineage of a marital relationship between Ruth and Boaz. Ruth believed that God was her ruler, sustainer, and healer. Oh Yes! Ruth lived a promising and productive life. God was Ruth's everything.

Their parochial society allowed Elkanah to marry another woman. He married another woman named Peninnah, and it appears that every time Elkanah looked at her, she became pregnant.

Peninnah, Elkanah, and Hannah were members of a love triangle. Elkanah married Hannah first, but she could not have any children or a son. A son was valued in that patriarchal society. If anything happened to the father, his son was obligated to help care for his Mother. So, Hannah was barren, but she wanted a son who could have one. But Elkanah loved Hannah more than he did Peninnah, which caused Peninnah to be highly jealous of Hannah.

Now, Hannah prayed about what she was going through. She wanted a child and a son, in particular, to carry for the family name. When I was married, my wife gave birth to our daughter. I was happy and excited that God blessed us with a healthy bouncing daughter. She was a pretty baby, and we loved her dearly because we ended up spoiling her.

Later, I asked my wife about us having another child and a son. If we had a son, I wanted to name him after me. Well. God blessed us eventually with a son. He became my name's sake. Hannah wanted a son, but she had a physical handicap that prevented her from giving birth. You know, all of us have some handicaps.

Despite her handicap condition, Hannah kept on praying to God. She was a faithful Mother who prayed. She did not allow her husband or her pastor, Eli to discourage her. Listen to what Hannah said to Elkanah and her Pastor, Ely.

I hear Hannah saying, "Elkanah, my darling, the fact that I cannot have any children and a boy is tarrying me apart. I cannot eat. I cannot sleep. I sometimes cry. The meditation that I am taking is not doing me any good".

Elkanah remarks, "Hannah, My Baby, My Darling, you know that I love you. I have told you that I love you on endless occasions and that I truly love you. I give you more than I give to Peninnah". Now, in all honesty, material things are not necessarily meaningful. Money and material things do not guarantee happiness.

Elkanah did not precisely understand what Hannah needed from him. Could it be that Elkanah was not sensitive enough to Hannah?

I can see Hannah walking down the street to the Shiloh Baptist Church. She went to have a solitary prayer and talk with Pastor Eli. After her prayer,

Pastor Eli says, "Hannah, I saw you praying, but I did not see you moving your lips. I know the liquor stores are not open, but Sister Hannah, Are you drunk?"

Now, Can I put a pen right here? I need to ask Pastor Eli one question. "Are you not a sanctified prophet and spirit-filled preacher? So, how do you know what time the liquor store opens? Have you been tiptoeing down to the liquor store to buy liquor"?

Can I tell you a secret? Preachers and Pastors are humans. They have feelings. They get hurt. They have heartbreaks. They even cry sometimes. They have problems sometimes. I knew of a preacher who was a son of a preacher. He had been raised in the church. He became a pastor when he was about 20 years of age. He was truly an outstanding preacher.

His Daddy died. Then, his home church called him to become their pastor. He accepted the call to become the pastor of his home church. He ended up pastoring two full-time churches. Although he had two churches, this pastor came under more pressure and stress. He developed a handicap condition called dipsomania. What does this mean? It means that we must also pray for our pastors and every preacher. We all need prayer.

Now, Pastor Eli did not understand what Hannah was going through. And, neither did her husband, Elkann, understand what Hannah was going through. In all seriousness, men did not understand what it was like to be a woman. Women and men are different.

The United States Supreme Court overturned the Rove v. Wade Case. Now that the Supreme Court overturned the Rove v Wade Case, this greatly impacts every state throughout America. Currently, man state legislatures throughout our nation are composed chiefly of men. But, right now, many state legislatures are telling women what they can and cannot do with their bodies. This is a social reality. Yes! And This is why Women need to vote. And this is why we all need to vote in every election.

Now, I like what Sister Hannah did. She knew neither Pastor Eli nor her husband, Elkann, understood what was happening with her body. They were men, and they were not women. So, Sister Hannah decided to take control and take charge of her body. She prayed to God, saying,

"Lord, you know me. You know everything about me. You know where I live. You know my street address. You know my private telephone number. But I need you every hour. What a friend we have in Jesus; All our sins and griefs to bear What a privilege to carry; Everything to God in prayer; Oh, what peace we often forfeit; Oh, what needless pain we bear; All because we do not carry Everything to God in prayer; Have we trials and temptations?; Is there trouble anywhere?; We should never be discouraged; Take it to the Lord in prayer Can we find a friend so faithful? Who will all our sorrows share? Jesus knows our every weakness; Take it to the Lord in prayer.

Hannah refused to keep quiet about her condition. She did what she could do for herself. But Hannah believed that she had a friend in God. She took all her concerns and cares to God in prayer.

Is this why the songwriter's song, "I won't complain"?

I've had some good days
I've had some hills to climb
I've had some weary days
And some sleepless nights
But when I, when I look around
And I think things over
All of my good days
Outweigh my bad days
I, I won't complain
Sometimes the clouds hang low
I can hardly see the road
I ask a question, Lord
Lord, why so much pain?

But He knows what's best for me
Although my weary eyes
They can't see
So I'll just say thank You, Lord
I, I won't complain

The Lord as been so good to me (Has He been good?)
He's been good to me
More than this whole world or you could ever be
He's been so good to me
You know what He did?
He, He dried all of my tears away
Turned my midnights into day
So I'll just say thank you, Lord
I've been lied on
But thank You, Lord
I've been talked about
But thank You, Lord
I've been misunderstood
But thank You Lord
You might be sick
Body wracked with pain
But thank You, Lord

Hannah was a faithful Mother. Regardless of what other people were saying to her or saying about her, Hannah prayed endlessly that God would somehow bless her with a child named Samuel. And God blessed her to give birth to Samuel. Samuel became one of the most acclaimed preachers in the history of Israel. Samuel had a faithful Mother who prayed. His Mother knew that God was always faithful. Oh Yes! God is faithful.

That you were wounded for my transgressions
You were bruised for my iniquities
By your stripes I'm already healed
So right then I dropped to my knees

And I called Jesus
He was right there
He heard my cry
He answered my prayer
He is faithful
He's been better to me
Than I been to myself
God is faithful
Yes God's faithful
And if God said it
It will come to pass
God is faithful
Oh yes God's faithful
Oh!
If God said it
I believe it
I don't doubt it
I receive it!
God is faithful, yes God's faithful
The Lord is faithful
My God is faithful, my God is faithful.

Esther 4:10-16

CHALLENGED TO MAKE A DIFFERENCE

I want to preach this morning on the subject "Challenged to Make a Difference." My subject comes from the book of Esther, Chapter Four Verses 10 through 16. It reads, "Then Esther spoke to Hathach and gave him a command for Mordecai. All the king's servants and the people of the king's provinces know that any man or woman who goes into the inner court to the inner court to the king who has not been called has but one law: put all to death, except the one to whom the king holds out the golden scepter, that he may live. Yet I have not been called to go into the king these thirty days". So, they told Mordecai Esther's words. And Mordecai told them to answer Esther, "Do not think in your heart that you will escape in the king's place anymore than all the other Jews. If you remain completely silent at this time, relief and deliverance will arise for the Jews from another place, but you and your father's house will perish. Yet who knows whether you have come to the kingdom for such a time as this?" Then Esther told them to reply to Mordecai. Go, gather all the Jews in Shushan, and fast for me; neither eat nor dirk for three days, night or day. My maids and I will fast likewise, And so I will go to the King, which is against the law; and if I perish, I perish" (Esther 4:10-16).

Queen Vashti was one of many strong and courageous women mentioned in the scriptures. Queen Vashi was a beautiful, intelligent, and classy kind of woman. She has been married to King Ahasuerus of Perish for some time.

But, one day, King Ahasuerus had some of his big-shot friends at his castle. King Ahasuerus wanted Queen Vashti to do something special for his friends. He wanted Vashti to parade and show how beautiful she was from her head down to her toes. Now, Queen Vashi sent this word back to, King Ahasuerus, "No. My Darling, I will not display, demonstrate, and illustrate my body to other men. My body, my hips, my breast, and my thighs are primarily for you only to see and romance me in our bedroom". Oh Yes! Queen Vashti was a proud and bold feminist who believed that she and her physician and no longer else, must have total control of her body.

Therefore, Queen Vashti rejected King Ahasuerus's idiotic and misogynistic request. He wanted her to do something which was totally against her values and morals. to simply embarrass her. But Queen Vashti's actions completely humiliated and infuriated the King. Queen Vashti's actions caused King Ahasuerus to look like a weak man who was not in charge of his wife or his household. So, in the midst of this difficult situation, King Ahasuerus divorced Vashti. Can you believe that?

Sometime after that, Ahasuerus became very lonely, and he decided to have a beautiful contest to select his next Queen of Shushan. Mordecai was an employee of King

Ahasuerus. And, Mordecai had a gorgeous-looking first cousin who was named Esther. At a young age, Esther's parents died. So, because of her parent's untimely death, Mordecai became Esther's guardian. He raised Esther as one of his own children. Now, in the process, Mordecai convinced Esther to participate in this beauty contest on behalf of King Ahasuerus; but Mordecai advised Esther not to reveal her Jewish identity.

Now, Esther enters the contest to become the Queen of Shushan. It was a very lengthy beauty contest, but of all the contestants who entered Esther won this beauty contest. She became Queen Shushan and King Ahasuerus's new wife. And the rest is now history.

Queen Esther's first cousin, Mordecai has an unfortunate confrontation. He had a confrontation with a man named Haman. Haman was the second most powerful person in Persia. But Haman had a problem with Mordecai. Mordecai refused to bow down to Haman every time he came by. Mordecai's religion prohibited him from bowing down to any man. The only person that Mordecai bowed down to was God.

Now, Can I put a pin here? I just stop by to tell you this. The only person who we are to bow down to is God. We must not bow down to any human being man or woman. We must not bow down to anyone in heaven or earth. But, we are to only bow down to God our maker and our creator.

Since Mordecai refused to bow down to him, Haman became bitter and vindicative towards Mordecai, and all people of Jewish people of Persia. So, Haman wanted to show Mordecai and all the Jewish people of Persia that he had the power to do whatever he wanted too. Next, Haman goes to King Ahasuerus to ask him for a favor, specifically. Haman's favor was simply evil and demonic.

You know, I must be completely honest here. We must watch our attitude and our actions. Sometimes we can become simply evil and demonic, especially when we get power in our hands. That is what happened on January 6. The people who had power in their hands decided to prevent the peaceful and orderly transfer of power.

So, because Haman power in his hand, Haman asked King Ahasuerus to make a decree to put to death of all Jewish people throughout Persia. If we do not watch ourselves, Power can absolutely corrupt us.

Haman was anti-Semitic, and this clearly reveals somethings. This clearly reveals that Adolph Hitler, Donald Trump, and Kanye West were not the first people to show their anti-Semitic beliefs and attitudes. Haman helped to pave the way for antisemitic in Persia and throughout the world.

Mordecai subsequently sent word to Queen Esther for her to take some immediate steps to help save their people. Mordecai said, "Esther, you must leave your safety zone. This edit that King Ahasuerus signed directly affects you. Do not think that because you are in the king's house, you, alone of all the Jews will escape. If you remain silent at this time, relief and deliverance for the Jews will arise from another place, but you and your father's family will perish. And who knows but that you have come to royal position for such a time as this" (Esther 4:12-14).

Now, the setting of this text is precise. Esther here is challenged right now to make a difference where she was. Esther has a challenge. And we must ask "How did

Esther decide to make a difference? Did Esther decide to make a difference by first preaching the first resurrection sermon? The first resurrection sermon was preached by Mary Madelene. Mary preached that I saw when Jesus was placed on the Cross at Calvary. The Roman Soldiers placed a crown of thorn on his head. They took shear and struck the spear into Jesus side. The blood of Jesus soared the ground of Golgotha. Jesus died and was placed tomb of Joseph of Artemia. But, three days later, on early Sunday morning, Mary Madelene preached the first resurrection sermon. No. Esther did not make a difference by preaching the firs resurrection sermon. Mary Madelene did that.

Did Esther choose to make a difference by running and winning in the World Olympics as a Tennessee State Tiger Bell? No. Instead, It was Wilma Rudolph from Clarksville, Tennessee who won the 100-yard sprint and 200-yard sprint races in Rome, Italy, and Wilma Rudolph, the Tennessee State Tiger Bell was called the world fastest woman.

Did Esther choose to make a difference by writing a book called *Courage to Be*? No. Paul Tillich, the Existentialist Philosopher and Theologian, wrote the book *Courage to Be*. Tillich said that we must take the courage to be what God has called us to be. We must not let anyone or any situation keep us from having the courage to be. So, Esther did not decide to write a book called *Courage to Be*.

Did Esther choose to make a difference by not starting the Montgomery Bus Protest in Montgomery, Alabama? Rosa Parks decided one day that she had enough of being discriminated against because of her skin color. Rosa Parks decided to ignore the segregation and discrimination laws of Montgomery. She did not get up and give her bus seat to a White person. Now, because of her civil disobedience, Rosa Parks was arrested and started the Montgomery Bus Protest. This Montgomery Bus Protest lasted for more than three (300) days. No! Esther did not decide to start the Montgomery Bus Protest.

Did Esther decide to make a difference by working as the Black Moses to lead her people from slavery in the South to freedom in the North? Harriet Tubman was the Black Moses of our people. Harriet Tubman led more than three (300) slaves out of slavery to freedom in the North. No! Esther did not decide to become the Black Moses. Harriet Tubman did that.

Did Esther choose to make a difference by getting on the Democratic ticket with President Joe Biden to become the first female Vice president of the United States? No. Esther did not become the first female Vice President. Kamal Harris became the first female Vice President of the United States.

Did Esther choose to make a difference by developing the Scientific Theory of Relativity? No. Albert Einstein is the scientist who developed the ingenious theory of relativity and dynamics.

Did Esther choose to make a difference by marrying Barack Obama and becoming the first African-American First Lady? No. Michelle Obama married Barack Obama and became the first woman of color to become the First Lady in the history of the United States.

Well. Here is how Esther chooses to make a difference for her people. She saw there was a fire within her house and heritage. Her people were about to be completely destroyed and annihilated. Esther says, "Cousin Mordecai, "I will do whatever I must do to save the lives of our people. Gather together all the Jews who are in Susah and fast for me. Do not eat or drink for three days, night or day. My maids and I will fast as you do when this is done. I will go to the King, even though it is against the law. And if I "perish, I perish" (Esther 4:15-16).

Now, Esther faced the possibility and penalty of death. Not even the Queen was to come before the King unannounced. If she had come before the King unannounced, Queen Esther could have been killed. Esther decides nonetheless to act to save the lives of her people. Esther did essentially what any loving woman would do. She sacrificed her life to save the lives of her people.

We can learn much from Esther life and experience. We can learn from Esther that no manner who we are or where we are, we can make a difference. We are challenge to make a difference in your home, on your job, in your community, and in your church. We can learn from Esther that to make a difference, we must always keep our hands in the hand of God. Did you hear what I said? We must always keep our hands in the God's hand. God hands are bigger than our hands. With God, we can do everything but fail. With God can always make a difference.

Oh Yes! I know a man who made a difference—and I want to talk about him for a minute, and maybe you will discover who I'm talking about as I go down the way because he made a difference. And he just went about serving. He was born in an obscure village, the child of a poor peasant woman. And then he grew up in still another obscure town, where he worked as a carpenter until he was thirty years old. Then for three years, he just got on his feet and was an itinerant preacher. And he went about making a difference. He didn't have much. He never wrote a book. He never held an office. He never had a family. He never held an office. He never had a Family. He never owned a house. He never went two hundred miles from where he was born. He did none of the usual things that the world would notice. He had no credentials but himself.

He was only thirty-three when the tide of public opinion turned against him. They called him a rabble-rouser. They him called a troublemaker. They said he was an agitator. He practiced civil disobedience. He was arrested. And he was turned over to his enemies and went through the mockery of a trial. And the irony of it all is that his friends turned him over to them. One of his close friends denied him. Another of his friends turned him over to his enemies. And while he was dying, the people who killed him gambled for his clothing, the possession that he had in the world. When he was dead, he was buried in a borrowed tomb, through the pity of a friend.

Twenty centuries have come and gone and today, he stands as the most influential figure ever in human history. All of the armies that ever marched, all the navies that ever sailed, all the parliaments that ever sat, and the kings that ever reigned put together have not affected the life of man on this earth as much as that one solitary life. His name may be a familiar one. But today I can hear them talking about him. Now and then, somebody says, He's King of Kings.

And again, I can hear somebody saying, "He Lord of Lords. Somewhere else I can hear somebody saying In Christ there is no East nor West. And then they go on and talk about, In him there's no North and South, but one

great Fellowship of Love throughout the whole wide world."
He didn't have anything. He just went around serving and
making a difference.

    Jesus, I tell you has made a difference in my life.

If it wasn't for the Lord, where would I be?
My life was nothing until He set me free.
What a change He made in my life,
no more compromising the wrong for the right.
(He made the difference),
(He made the difference in my life).

He gives me joy that cannot be surpassed,
I'm on a cloud from the first moment to the last
He walks with me, talks with me,
telling me I'm His own.
He calms all my fears,
telling me I am not alone.

I don't walk like I used to walk,
He made the difference.
I don't talk like I used to talk,
He made the difference.
I don't live like I used to live,
He made the difference.
I don't give like I used to give,
He made the difference.
He made the difference,
He made the difference in my life.

Near the cross of Jesus stood His mother, His mother's sister, Mary the wife of Clopas, and Mary Magdalene. When Jesus, saw His mother there, and the disciple whom He loved standing nearby, He said to her mother, "Woman, here is your son," and to the disciple, "Here is your mother!" And from that time on, this disciple took her into his own home (John 19: 25-27).

The Dear Momma Experience

To my good friend and brother, Dr. Joseph Clayborne, the officers and members of Boston Baptist Church, and my sisters, brothers, and friends. I can assure you it would take me the rest of my days to live up to this charming congregation member's eloquent, beautiful introduction. It makes me feel very humble. And such encouraging words give me renewed courage and vigor to continue our constant struggle for justice, equality, and human dignity. I'm deeply grateful to your esteemed pastor for extending my invitation to be with you. And I'm thankful to him for the support that he gives me and my entire family. I learned a long time ago that you can't make it by yourself in this world. You need friends, somebody to pat you on the back; you need somebody to give you consolation in the darkest hour.

Our beloved Mother, Mother Elizabeth Murphy-Clayton, was a member of this loving congregation for over fifty (50) years. She had a long history of loving every one of Boston Baptist Church. She loved Pastor Oris Mays, his wife, and their family. She loved Pastor Ishmael and his family. Also, our Mother loved Pastor

Clayborne, his devoted wife, his charming family, and all the members of Boston Baptist Church. So, I am eternally grateful to my children, siblings, nieces, nephews, other family members, and friends for their kind support and encouragement throughout my years of trying to preach the gospel.

This morning, I want to remind you that this is Mother's Day. But for me, I believe that every day ought to be Mother's Day. Every Mother is remarkable. I did not worship my Mother because I am a believer. I only worship God. But I did worship the ground my Mother walked because she walked on holy ground. Our Mother paved the way for me, my sisters, and my brothers. My life is better because of the sacrifice that my Mother made for me. So, if you do not mind, I want to talk to you about "The Dear Momma Experience."

This subject has gardened and grabbed my attention because of the relationship that Jesus experienced with his beloved Mother, Mary. Let me now read about this relationship from the gospel of John chapter nineteen, verses twenty-five through twenty-seven.

I must be honest with you, my sisters, brothers, and friends. This particular scripture, particularly in John Chapter nineteen, verses 25 through 27, strikes me, grabs me, touches me, and causes me to get extremely emotional. It is one of the last seven words of Jesus from his cross on Calvary. He says, (1) Father, forgive them; for they know not what they do; (2) Today shalt thou be with me in paradise; (3) My God, my God, why hast thou forsaken me; (4) I thirst.; (5) It is finished; (6) Father, into thy hands I commend my spirit, and (7) Woman, here is your son."

Jesus was nailed to his cross on Calvary. Oh Yes! Jesus is experiencing terrible, unforgettable, and unbearable pain. It is here also that Jesus is, yes extremely emotional. He speaks his last words to his disciples, and most importantly, Jesus speaks his last words to his loving Mother.

I become highly emotional and moved whenever I think, speak, or talk about my loving and devoted Mother. About four (4) months ago, I stood at my Mother's bedside. My sincere and loving Mother breathed her last breath. I spoke my last words to my Mother. I call this the Dear Momma Experience. The Gangster Rapper 2pac Shakur has a song called "Dear Momma, You Are Appreciated". When I was sick as a little kid, To keep me happy, there's no limit to the things you did, And all my childhood memories, Are full of all the sweet things you did for me, And even though I act crazy, I gotta thank the Lord that you made me".

Based on our New Testament text, we can equally speak about the Dear Momma Experience in several ways. Firstly, we can consider what Jesus went through on his cross at Calvary. Jesus has his Dear Momma's Experience. He speaks ultimately to his loving Mother, Mary.

But, before speaking to her, Jesus says to his other disciples. He speaks to his Beloved disciple, Mary, the wife of Clopas, and Mary Magdalene. The Beloved disciple's name is mentioned several times in the New Testament, especially throughout the gospel of John. The beloved disciple is there when Jesus told his disciples, "One of you will betray me." The beloved disciple was there when the women preached the first resurrection

When Dr. Taylor was a young teenager at thirteen years of age, his father, who was also a Baptist pastor, died suddenly. When he got the news about his father's death, it was got up early one morning. He stood outside his Momma's bedroom door. As he stood there, Gardner Taylor said, "Momma, what are we going to do? Daddy is gone home to be with the Lord. And his loving Momma responds, "Gardner, my son, I want you to know the Lord will make a way somehow."

Now, nearly fifty years later, Dr. Garden Taylor preached a sermon. I heard him say, "Yesterday afternoon. I stood at my Momma's gravesite in the Evergreen Cemetery. I said to her dust, "Thank you, (Momma). The Lord will make a way somehow; yes, God will. I do not know how, but I know who. I've been in the storm so long now, on the sea and in the air.

I don't know how I've come through, but I know who; yes, I do. I know who has brought me all this journey. I know Who, Who has directed our pathways. I know Who. I can't tell you this morning how you'll get through whatever you face, but I know who can get you safely through. I know Who can pick you up when you fall down. I know Who can straighten you out when you're wrong. I know who can comfort you when you're sad. I know who a friend will be when you've got no friends. I know who will dry the tears in your eyes. I know Who. The Lord will make a way; oh yes, God will. The Lord will make a way, somehow. Never mind about how if you know Who. I know "all things work together for our good for those who love God" (Romans 8:28).

I want you to understand clearly that the Dear Momma Experience is personal. And, if you keep on living, I just stopped by to tell you this. One day, you will have your own Dear Momma Experience. Not too long ago, I had my Dear Momma Experience. I stood at the bedside of my loving Momma. My Momma was in Hospice Care and her home. She was spending her last days at her home.

She said to me, all her children and grandchildren, "When it is time for God to call me home. I do not want you all to worry about me. I got my business straight with God a long time ago. I know where I am going. I am going home to meet my God and meet my Savior. When God calls me, I want God to call me to come home from the house God has blessed me for over forty years.

My Momma lay there dying. My baby brother and I stood at her bedside. Within my mind and my heart, I took a spiritual flight with God. I sang an old song and prayed a prayer. I sang "This may be my last time. This may be my last time. This may be my last time. This may be the last time that we will ever sing together; I do not know". Then, I prayed, "Dear God. I thank you for my Momma. I thank you for my Father. I thank you for our ancestors. They worked and sacrificed so that succeeding generations would have a better life.

I kept praying: "Dear Momma, Dear Momma, Dear Momma. You gave me sometimes your last dollar, and you did not know sometimes where you would get your next penny. Because of your sacrifice, we made it through some hard days. Some days, we did not have enough food to eat. Some days we did not have the best clothes to wear. Some days, we did not have heat to warm our bodies from cold winter nights.

I kept on praying. Momma, God knows that, as a family, we made it through some hard and difficult days. And, my Momma, God blessed Your nine children because of your many sacrifices. Your nine children were able to get a good education. Your nine children studied at some of the best institutions in the world. "Study to show yourself approve a workman is not ashamed rightfully dividing the word of truth "(2 Timothy 2:15).

You know my sisters and my brothers; Momma taught us so much. She taught us the value of a good education. Momma also taught us to never look down on those who could not get an education. Whenever we look down on other people, it speaks volumes about our character and our integrity. Now, "Do you know that some people look down on people who were unable to get a good quality education? Dr. Martin Luther King Jr was a highly educated clergyman and Baptist preacher. He matriculated through some of the most prestigious educational institutions in our world.

However, like my devoted Mother, Dr. King criticized people and preachers who looked down on others. He said, "I remember when I was in theological school, and we were coming to the end of our years there, a classmate came to me to talk with me and said he wanted to invite his mother up. And she'd struggled to help him get through school. He wanted to invite his mother up, but said, "You know, the problem is I don't know if she would quite fit in this atmosphere. You know, her verbs aren't quite right, and she doesn't know how to dress too well; she lives in a rural area". And I want to tell him you aren't fit to finish this school. If you cannot acknowledge your mother, if you cannot acknowledge your brothers and sisters, even if they have not risen to the heights of education attainment, then you aren't fit to go out and try to preach to men, women (and children)".

Oh Yes! I learned so much from my devoted and loving Momma. I do not have enough time to tell you how much I learned from her and what I learned from her. I learned more truth from my Momma on her knees than from the philosopher on his tiptoes. Oh Yes! I learned another thing from my darling Momma. Yes. I learned, "When a man finds a wife, he finds what is good and receives favor from the LORD (Proverbs 18:22). Did you hear what I just said? Let me repeat that. I learned from my devoted Momma, "When a man finds a wife, he finds what is good and receives favor from the Lord." Do I have a witness?

Dear Momma, Dear Momma. Oh Yes! It has taken me a long time, but I can now finally understand the meaning of this poem. You taught me this poem by Langton Hughes, "Mother to Son."

Well, son, I'll tell you:
Life for me ain't been no crystal stair.
It's had tacks in it,
And splinters,
And boards torn up,
And places with no carpet on the floor—
Bare.

But all the time
I'se been a-climbin' on,
And reachin' landin's,
And turnin' corners,
And sometimes goin' in the dark
Where there ain't been no light.
So boy, don't you turn back.
Don't you set down on the steps
'Cause you finds it's kinder hard.
Don't you fall now—
For I'se still goin', honey,
I'se still climbin',
And life for me ain't been no crystal stair.

Dear Momma. Dear Momma, I am coming home now. Dear Momma, We learned from your own noble, moral, and spiritual examples what it means to be an American patriot truly. Your five sons served this great nation. They put their lives in harm's way, volunteered to put their lives in danger, and they served honorably in the United States military for God and their Country.

Dear Momma, Dear Momma, Dear Momma. You always gave us the special love and attention that we needed. You always cheer us on with inspiring words, prayers, and songs. Do you not know that,

I'll always love my Mama
She's my favorite girl
I'll always love my Mama
She brought me into this world
Sometimes I feel so bad

When I think of all the things, I used to do
How Mama used to clean somebody else's house
Just to buy me a new pair of shoes
I never understood how Mama made it through the week
When she never ever got a good night's sleep
Talking 'bout mama
She's one of a kind
Talking 'bout mama
You've got your yours, and I've got mine
Talking 'bout mama
Oh, hey Mama, hey Mama, my heart belongs to you
I'll always love my mama
She's my favorite girl
You only get one, you only get one, yeah
I'll always love my mama
She brought me into this world
A mother's love is so special
It's something that you can't describe
It's the kind of love that stays with you
Until the day you die
She taught me little things like "Say Hello and Thank you, please"
While scrubbing those floors on her bended knees
Talking 'bout mama
She's one of a kind
Talking 'bout mama
You've got your yours and I've got mine
I'll always love my mama
She's my favorite girl

burial. You will always have the poor among you, but you will not always have me".

The setting is crystal clear. Mary did something extremely unusual. She was the sister of Martha and Lazarus. She demonstrated her love and devotion to Jesus and Jesus's ministry. Mary understood that something drastic was about to happen to Jesus. Within the next few days, Jesus would be arrested on some trumped-up charges that he was guilty of committing blasphemy and healing a sick man on the sabbath day. So, Mary decided to illustrate her support and abiding admiration for Jesus's ministry. She took out this expensive bottle of perfume. While he reclined in a chair, Jesus's feet were elevated. Mary took this costly perfume and poured it out on Jesus' feet. Then, she took her long hair to dry his feet.

Now, Judas Iscariot objected to what Mary did. He argued, complained, and criticized Mary. I hear him saying, "Mary, you should not have done what you have done. This expensive perfume could have been used to sell to buy some food for the poor".

Now, very quickly, we are very familiar with people like Judas. No matter what we do, whether it is good, bad, or indifferent, somebody will criticize us. Dr. Gardner Taylor and Dr. Benjamin Mays offer some insight here. Gardner Taylor said that his church building, where he served as the Senior Pastor, was severely damaged several years ago. It had been damaged by fire. So, his congregation temporarily relocated to another location. They began to hold services there. One of Reverend Taylor's church leaders became highly critical and negative at that time. This critic stated to Pastor Taylor 'we will probably lose many members. But, instead of losing members, Pastor Taylor said his church membership increased significantly.

Dr. Benjamin Mays said something about Judas Iscariot that I shall never forget. He preached a sermon called "Let us be kind to Judas." Dr. Mays wanted us to be kind to Judas Iscariot because there is some Judas in all of us. We have all intentionally or unintentionally betrayed someone.

We turn our attention to what Mary did with her hair. Indeed, what she did was unusual. She took some expensive oil from its container. Took this oil. Rubbed it on Jesus' feet. Then, she used her long hair to dry his feet. Simultaneously, we begin to think about our own use of hair.

When I was a teenager, I tried always to be a teenager who had himself together. I majored in looking good and dressing well. I worked a job in the evening and on weekends throughout most of my high school and college career. I quit playing high school basketball to work a job. I needed to work to help my beloved and loving mother. She was a single parent and the head of the household. Besides me, she had eight other children to provide for. They were four daughters and four other sons. So, I needed to quit playing basketball to work a full-time job at night. I worked to help Momma take care of her household.

Now, whenever I had a few extra dollars left over, I would buy expensive clothes and other attire. I always tried to dress to impress the young ladies and my friends. So, with this in mind, I remember it became fashionable for my male friends and me to get our hair permed. I tried calling my hair permed only once. I allowed my friend Clarence Murchison put perm my hair.

Clarence had his hair perm, and he was making some money. Although he was not a barber, my friends and I allowed Clarence to perm our hair for a small price. Right now, I am bald. But, at that time, I wore an Afro hairstyle. My hair was kinky, tall, and longer than usual. Then, I had my hair permed.

James Brown and Al Sharpton are also very concerned about how their hair looks. James Brown was called the number one Soul Brother. He was always obsessed with ensuring he looked perfect, and his hair was the most critical aspect of his style. James Brown proclaimed, "*Hair is the first thing. And teeth are the second thing. Hair and teeth. A man got those two things. He's got it all.*"

His wife revealed that even in old age, when his **hair was thinning**, James Brown needed to ensure it looked great. In a recent interview, his wife said, "*I would spend hours doing his hair because he wouldn't leave the house until he had his 'James Brown hair'.*

Al Sharpton met James Brown during his days as a street preacher in Harlem and leader of a civil rights organization for youths. Sharpton became friends with Teddy Brown, one of James Brown's sons. Unfortunately, Teddy was killed in a car accident. James Brown flew to New York to attend his son's funeral and James Brown asked to meet the young minister who had befriended his son. Brown eventually assumed the role of mentor and father figure to Al Sharpton. Sharpton had been raised in the projects by his single mother whose own father had abandoned him.

Sharpton idolized Brown. Brown was a world celebrity and happened to wear perms that could rival any woman's hairdo. When Brown decided he wanted Sharpton to abandon his Afro and get a hairstyle that resembled his own, no questions were asked. Brown received an invitation from President Ronald Reagan to discuss making Dr. Martin Luther King's birthday a national holiday.

Brown invited Sharpton to accompany him, but Brown wanted him to get his hair done for the occasion. James Brown took Sharpton to his hairdresser, who permed his hair. Al Sharpton's hair has been that way ever since.

I thoroughly enjoy reading. I read that the philosophers Plato and Aristotle used to stay up until late every night. They would argue about the merits of men with short-cropped hair combined with a heard. Plato and Aristotle also had their opinion about how men ought to wear their hair.

The psychoanalyst talks about sometimes what do about our hair. Alfred Adler and Sigmund Freud are just two (2) psychoanalysts who come to mind. Alfred Adler insisted that we all have the desire for attention. So, to get some attention, we get our hair cut and taken care of. We make regular appointments with our cosmetologist and or barber shop. We must do something with our hair because we desire to get attention.

Sigmund Freud talked and discussed that we have three parts to our personality. These personality traits include the id, ego, and super-ego. They interact to form a whole within us, and the id, ego, and super-ego each part make a relative contribution to an individual's behavior. So, according to Sigmund Freud, This is why we want our hair to look good. We must satisfy our id, ego, and super-ego.

Now, eventually, I am going to get to what Jesus has to say about the use proper use of our hair. But let me say a few

But they can't touch
My inner mystery.
When I try to show them,

They say they still can't see
I say,
It's in the arch of my back,
The sun of my smile,
The ride of my breasts,
The grace of my style.
I'm a woman
Phenomenal woman,
That's me.

Samson had a concern about the proper use of his hair. His might and strength were in his hair. But tragically, Samson got caught in the web of a phenomenal woman. Her name was Delilah.

Chris Rock did a documentary called "Good Hair." Lola and Zahra are his two young daughters. Lola asked him, "Daddy, why don't you have good hair? Like so many people, Lola and Zahra thought that good hair was white people's hair. So, Lola and Zahra, Chris Rock's daughters, challenged him with their question about Good Hair. To address their question intelligently and responsibly, Chris Rock developed a documentary entitled "Good Hair."

Is this why some women do not want their husband or anyone else to touch their hair? They are concerned about their Good Hair. I saw a television interview with an attractive African American woman. She expressed an interesting opinion about her hair. She said that her significant other was forbidden to touch her hair.

Now, Jesus noticed Mary was unconcerned about who touched her hair. Jesus said, "Mary, you used your hair for a noble purpose. You used your hair to illustrate your purpose for living. You used your hair. I give thanks to God. You used your hair to receive an unexpected blessing from God. You used your hair to say I give praise, honor, and glory to God.

You use your hair to say, "Trust in the LORD with all thine heart And lean not unto thine own understanding. In all your ways acknowledge God, and God shall direct our path (Proverbs 3:5- 6).

You use your hair to say, "The Lord is my light and my salvation; Whom shall I fear? The Lord is the strength of my life; Of whom shall I be afraid? When the wicked came against me To eat up my flesh. My enemies and foes. They stumbled and fell. However, an army may encamp against me. My heart shall not fear, Though war may rise against me. In this will be confident. One thing I have desired of the Lord that I will seek. That I may dwell in the house of the Lord" (Psalm 27:1-3).

I have learned from Mary of Bethan always to use my hair to give praise, honor, and glory to what God has done through Jesus Christ.

John 19:25-27

THE DEAR MOMMA EXPERIENCE

Near the cross of Jesus stood His mother, His mother's sister, Mary the wife of Clopas, and Mary Magdalene. When Jesus, saw His mother there, and the disciple whom He loved standing nearby, He said to her mother, "Woman, here is your son," and to the disciple, "Here is your mother!" And from that time on, this disciple took her into his own home (John 19:25-27).

The Dear Momma Experience

To my good friend and brother, Dr. Joseph Clayborne, the officers and members of Boston Baptist Church, and my sisters, brothers, and friends. It would take me the rest of my days to live up to this charming congregation member's eloquent, beautiful introduction. It makes me feel very humble. And such encouraging words give me renewed courage and vigor to continue our constant struggle for justice, equality, and human dignity. I'm deeply grateful to your esteemed pastor for extending my invitation to be with you. And I'm thankful to him for the support that he gives me and my entire family. I learned a long time ago that you can't make it by yourself in this world. You need friends, somebody to pat you on the back; you need somebody to give you consolation in the darkest hour.

Our beloved Mother, Mother Elizabeth Murphy-Clayton, was a member of this loving congregation for over fifty (50) years. She had a long history of loving everyone at Boston Baptist Church. She loved Pastor Oris Mays, his wife, and their family. She loved Pastor Ishmael and his family. Also, our Mother loved Pastor Clayborne, his devoted wife, his charming family, and all the members of Boston Baptist Church. So, I am eternally grateful to my children, siblings, nieces, nephews, other family members, and friends for their kind support and encouragement throughout my years of trying to preach the gospel.

This morning, I want to remind you that this is Mother's Day. But for me, I believe that every day ought to be Mother's Day. Every Mother is remarkable. I did not worship my Mother because I am a believer. I only worship God. But I did worship the ground my Mother walked because she walked on holy ground. Our Mother paved the way for me, my sisters, and my brothers. My life is better because of the sacrifice that my Mother made for me. So, if you do not mind, I want to talk to you about "The Dear Momma Experience."

This subject has gardened and grabbed my attention because of the relationship that Jesus experienced with his beloved Mother, Mary. Let me now read about this

financial supporters of his ministry. This same Mary Magdalene preached the first resurrection sermon. So, I ask everyone here to do me one kind favor. Please do not tell me that a woman cannot preach the gospel. It was a woman who preached the first resurrection sermon. She preached that Jesus was alive.

Most importantly, Jesus' devoted Mother Mary stands at his cross on Calvary. Jesus is dying, and he is about to breathe his last breath. Jesus's blood soaps his eyes, and blood soaps his entire body. Now, Jesus' entire attention is focused squarely on Mary, his Mother. Jesus has his Dear Momma experience. He says, "Woman, here is your son."

I call this the Dear Momma experience. I hear Jesus saying, "Momma, you taught me my ABCs. You taught me how to read and write. You taught me mathematics and calculus. You taught me the scriptures. This is why I preached with power, "The Spirit of the Lord is upon Me Because He has anointed Me To preach the gospel of the poor; He has sent Me to heal the brokenhearted." To proclaim liberty to the captives, And recovery of the sight to the blind, To set all liberty those who are bruised; To proclaim the acceptable year of the Lord."

Dear Momma, You taught me by your example how to believe and trust totally in God. You taught me by your example how to treat people how I wish to be treated. You taught me to never give up on people and always to love people. You taught me to study God's word and be completely transparent and truthful. "You shall know the truth, and the truth shall set you free" (John 8:32). I am about to breathe my last breath, but I do not want you to be worried about me. God will take care of me. I am in God's hands. Neither do I want you to be worthy of yourself because my beloved disciple will care for you for the rest of your days. Dear Momma, Dear Momma, Dear Momma.

Now, we can speak about the Dear Momma Experience because we know it is universal. Everyone will have their Dear Momma experience. Please allow me to share something about one of my preaching mentors. His name is Dr. Gardner C. Taylor. He served as the Concord Baptist Church of Christ's Senior Pastor for forty-two years in Brooklyn, New York. He has been called one of the greatest preachers who has ever lived. Dr. Rueben H. Green, my pastor, told me, Otis, whenever you get the opportunity, please hear Reverend Taylor preach.

When Dr. Taylor was a young teenager at thirteen years of age, his father, who was also a Baptist pastor, died suddenly. When he got the news about his father's death, it was got up early one morning. He stood outside his Momma's bedroom door. As he stood there, Gardner Taylor said, "Momma, what are we going to do? Daddy is gone home to be with the Lord. And his loving Momma responds, "Gardner, my son, I want you to know the Lord will make a way somehow."

Now, nearly fifty years later, Dr. Garden Taylor preached a sermon. I heard him say, "Yesterday afternoon. I stood at my Momma's gravesite in the Evergreen Cemetery. I said to her dust, "Thank you, (Momma). The Lord will make a way somehow; yes, God will. I do not know how, but I know who. I've been in the storm so long now, on the sea and in the air.

I don't know how I've come through, but I know who; yes, I do. I know who has brought me all this journey. I know Who, Who has directed our pathways. I know Who. I can't tell you this morning how you'll get through whatever you face, but I know who can get you safely through. I know Who can pick you up when you fall. I know Who can straighten you out when you're wrong. I know who can comfort you when you're sad. I know who a friend will be when you've got no friends. I know who will dry the tears in your eyes. I know Who. The Lord will make a way; oh yes, God will. The Lord will make a way, somehow. Never mind about how if you know Who. I know "all things work together for our good for those who love God" (Romans 8:28).

I want you to understand clearly that the Dear Momma Experience is personal. And, if you keep on living, I just stopped by to tell you this. One day, you will have your own Dear Momma Experience. Not too long ago, I had my Dear Momma Experience. I stood at the bedside of my loving Momma. My Momma was in Hospice Care at her home. She was spending her last days at her home.

She told me, all her children and grandchildren, "When it is time for God to call me home. I do not want you all to worry about me. I got my business straight with God a long time ago. I know where I am going. I am going home to meet my God and meet my Savior. When God calls me, I want God to contact me to come home from the house God has blessed me for over forty years.

My Momma lay there dying. My baby brother and I stood at her bedside. Within my mind and my heart, I took a spiritual flight with God. I sang an old song and prayed a prayer. I sang, "This may be my last time. This may be my last time. This may be my last time. This may be the last time we will ever sing together; I do not know". Then, I prayed, "Dear God. I thank you for my Momma. I thank you for my Father. I thank you for our ancestors. They worked and sacrificed so that succeeding generations would have a better life.

I kept praying: "Dear Momma, Dear Momma, Dear Momma. You gave me sometimes your last dollar, and you did not know sometimes where you would get your next penny. Because of your sacrifice, we made it through some hard days. Some days, we did not have enough food to eat. Some days, we did not have the best clothes to wear. Some days, we did not have heat to warm our bodies from cold winter nights.

I kept on praying. Momma, God knows that, as a family, we made it through some hard and difficult days. And, my Momma, God blessed Your nine children because of your many sacrifices. Your nine children were able to get a good education. Your nine children studied at some of the best institutions in the world. "Study to show yourself approve a workman is not ashamed rightfully dividing the word of truth "(2 Timothy 2:15).

You know my sisters and my brothers; Momma taught us so much. She taught us the value of a good education. Momma also introduced us to never look down on those who could not get an education. Whenever we look down on other people, it speaks volumes about our character and our integrity. Now, "Do you know that some people look down on people who could not get a good quality education? Dr. Martin Luther King Jr was a highly educated clergyman and Baptist preacher. He matriculated through some of the most prestigious educational institutions in our world.

However, like my devoted Mother, Dr. King criticized people and preachers who looked down on others. He said, "I remember when I was in theological school, and we were coming to the end of our years there, a classmate came to me to talk with me and said he wanted to invite his mother up. And she'd struggled to help him get through school. He wanted to invite his mother up but said, "You know, the problem is I don't know if she would quite fit in this atmosphere. You know, her verbs aren't quite right, and she doesn't know how to dress too well; she lives in a rural area". And I want to tell him you aren't fit to finish this school. If you cannot acknowledge your mother if you cannot acknowledge your brothers and sisters, even if they have not risen to the heights of education attainment, then you aren't fit to go out and try to preach to men, women (and children)".

Oh Yes! I learned so much from my devoted and loving Momma. I do not have enough time to tell you how much I learned from her and what I learned from her. I learned more truth from my Momma on her knees than from the philosopher on his tiptoes. Oh Yes! I learned another thing from my darling Momma. Yes. I knew, "When a man finds a wife, he finds what is good and receives favor from the LORD (Proverbs 18:22). Did you hear what I just said? Let me repeat that. I learned from my devoted Momma, "When a man finds a wife, he finds what is good and receives favor from the Lord." Do I have a witness?

Dear Momma, Dear Momma. Oh Yes! It has taken me a long time, but I can now finally understand the meaning of this poem. You taught me this poem by Langton Hughes, "Mother to Son."

Well, son, I'll tell you:
Life for me ain't been no crystal stair.
It's had tacks in it,
And splinters,
And boards torn up,
And places with no carpet on the floor—
Bare.
But all the time
I'se been a-climbin' on,
And reachin' landin's,
And turnin' corners,
And sometimes goin' in the dark
Where there ain't been no light.
So boy, don't you turn back.
Don't you set down on the steps
'Cause you finds it's kinder hard.
Don't you fall now—
For I'se still goin', honey,
I'se still climbin',
And life for me ain't been no crystal stair.

On her, you can depend
You can depend on a helping hand to lend
Your mother loves her children all the time
When children go away
A mother prays both night and day
Mother always keeps them resting on her mind
Oh, Yes. She's always on her knees crying
Lord have, have mercy, please
Your mother loves her children all the time.

Glory, Glory, Glory! Hallelujah. I thank God for my Momma. I thank God for all.

Mothers. Glory, Glory, Glory! Hallelujah.

John 20:1, 11–18

MARY MAGDALENE: OUR KIND OF A PREACHER

I want to preach this morning on the subject of "Mary Magdalene: Our Kind of a Preacher." My subject grows from the Gospel of Saint John Chapter 20, verses 1 and 11 through 18. I am reading from the New King James translation of scripture. It reads, "Now, on the first day of the week, Mary Magdalene went to the tomb early, while it was still dark, and saw that the stone had been taken away from the tomb." "But Mary Magdalene stood outside by the tomb weeping, and as she wept, she stooped down and looked into the tomb." And she saw two angels in white sitting one at the head and the other at the feet, where the body of Jesus had lain. Then they said to her: Woman, why are you weeping?" She said to them, "Because they have taken away my Lord, and I do not know where they had laid Him." Now, when she had said this, she turned around and saw Jesus standing there, and did not know that it was Jesus. Jesus said to her, "Woman, why are you weeping? Whom are you seeking?" She, supposing Him to be gardener, said to Him, "Sir, if you have carried Him away, tell me where You have laid Him, and I will take Him away". Jesus said to her, "Mary!" She turned and said to Him, "Rabbi (which is to say, Teacher). Jesus told her, "Do not cling to Me, for I have not yet ascended to My Father, but go to My brethren and say to them, I am ascending to My Father and your Father and to My God and your God. Mary Magdalene told the disciples that she had seen the Lord and that He had spoken these things to her".

The Southern Baptist Church Convention has excommunicated several churches from its convention. The churches that the Southern Baptist Church Convention excommunicated went against its rules and regulations. These excommunicated churches licensed, ordained, and installed women as pastors and preachers. Indeed, this Southern Baptist Church Convention position marks a complex and disturbing day within the entire body of Christ. I now realize that I was sadly mistaken. I had developed the idea, the notion, and the understanding that the body of Christ today was becoming more equalitarian. I thought that the church today was becoming more inclusive and not exclusive. I thought the church was increasingly accepting women in the ministry. I believe Women and Men are equal. "We all have sinned and come short of the glory of God" (Romans 3:23). There is neither Jew nor Greek, there is neither slave nor free, there is neither male nor female; for we are all one in Christ Jesus"(Galatians 3:28).

In the New Testament, we go back to the ministry of Apostle Paul and Jesus. In their churches, women play significant leadership roles. Women were teachers, deacons, pastors, and, yes, preachers. Lydia was a successful businesswoman. She sold purple fabric, possibly to men of the Omega Psi Phi Fraternity Incorporated. However, Lydia became a Christian through the teaching and preaching of Paul. Then, Lydia even organized and started a church in her home. Lydia can be considered one of the church's organizing pastors at Philippi (Acts 16:14-15).

So, I want you to know something here. Like you, I vehemently oppose the Southern Baptist Church Convention's position about women in ministry. I support women in all levels of ministry. Women, especially like Mary Magdalene, are our kind of preacher. Mary Madalene is an example of a powerful gospel preacher. Her powerful preaching is a direct product of Jesus's ministry.

Now, I must be crystal clear here. Mary Magdalene is not our kind of preacher, not because of what Lionel Richie and Commodores song about. They had a popular song called "Brick House".

Ow, she's a brick house
Well put-together, everybody knows
This is how the story goes
She knows she got everything
That a woman needs to get a man, yeah, yeah
How can she lose with the stuff she use
Thirty-six, twenty-four, thirty-six oh what a winning hand.

No! No! No! Mary Magdalene is not our kind of preacher because she is a Brick House. Let me suggest several reasons: "Why is Mary Magdalene our kind of preacher"? I noticed that Mary Magdalene is our kind of preacher because she financially supported the ministry of Jesus. Mary Magdalene matriculated from a wealthy community in the City of Magdala. The City of Magdala was located along the coast of the Sea of Galilee in modern-day Palestine. Do you remember what the gospel writer Luke reports about Mary Magdalene? Luke stated that Mary Magdalene was one of several women Jesus healed (Luke 8:1-3). What Jesus healed her of, we do not know exactly. God has also healed each one of something, but we do not know what God healed you of. You know that.

But here is one thing we do know. Mary Magdalene was a died-hard financial supporter of Jesus's ministry. She gave to the ministry of Jesus, and, when she gave, Mary Magdalene was not concerned about giving to Jesus' ministry before or after taxes. She just gave whatever she had.

The story is told that the deacon and ushers took up the tithes and offerings at this particular church. It was at the Sunday Morning Worship Service. The deacons and ushers passed the offering plate throughout the congregation. And as the offering plate was being passed around, this visitor at church did something unusual. This visitor decided to stand up inside the offering plate. So, the pastor stood up to ask this visitor one question. The Pastor says, "Sir, We do not have many offering plates. So, "Why are you standing up in the church offering plate? This visitor replied, "Brother Pastor, the only thing that I have to give is myself.

And this is precisely what Mary Magdalene gave to support the ministry of Jesus. She gave herself. I hear someone saying, "Give, and it shall be given unto you; good measure, pressed down and shaken together, and running over, will be put into your bosom. With the same measure you use, it will be measured back to you" (Luke 6:38-40). I hear someone saying, "Give as God purposes in your heart, not grudgingly or of necessity, for God loves a cheerful giver." (2 Cor 9:7). I hear someone saying, "If When you give the best of your service to the Lord telling the world that the Savior has come, be not dismayed when men do not believe you, God understands, and God will tell you well done., Good and faithful servant, well done". Mary Magdalene gave financially to support the ministry of Jesus.

Notice also that Mary Magdalene is our kind of preacher because she was a conscientious disciple in the ministry of Jesus. Every preacher in her or his mind ought to take preaching seriously. God people come to Church Sunday after Sunday and sometimes come to Church during the week. When God's people come to Church, they come to church with so many things on their minds. They have the world's weight on their shoulders. They are going through a divorce. They have lost loved ones to death. They have lost their jobs. They have children on drugs. They have loved ones and friends unfairly in jail. They are facing racism and discrimination because of the color of their skin. They are looking for love in the wrong places. They know

During the Civil Rights protest in Birmingham, Alabama, a deadly bomb destroyed a major portion of the 16th Street Baptist Church in Birmingham, Alabama. Unfortunately, in that bombing, four little girls were killed. There were: (1) Addie May Collins, (2) Carol Denise McNair, (3) Cynthia Wesley, and (4) Carole Rosamond Robertson. Reverend Martin Luther King, Jr preached their funerals. He was incredibly courageous and persuasive as he eulogized these four precious angles. Now, as he stood up to preach, he cried tears endlessly. Reverend King said, "Goodnight, sweet princesses; may the light of angels take thee to thy eternal rest." He cried. I do not know a preacher who does not cry about the pains, heartbreaks, and sufferings of God's people.

Also, at the gravesite of Jesus, Mary Magdalene demonstrated that she had a dedicated prayer life. She prayed about what she was going through. Mary Magdalene was grieving because she experienced the death of Jesus. So, She prayed. Through prayer, Mary Magdalene knew that God could help her overcome what she was going through.

Harry Emerson Fosdick was called one of the most outstanding preachers of the 20th century. He served as the Pastor of the Riverside Church in New York City. The multimillionaire John Rockefeller was one of the most faithful members of that congregation. But, despite the money in his pockets, John Rockefeller loved to hear the preaching of his pastor, Harry Emerson Fosdick.

Now, Fosdick had something to preach about. Years before becoming the Pastor at the Riverside Church, Fosdick temporarily lost his mind and was admitted into the insane asylum. While in the insane asylum, Fosdick got to know God more personally. He spent more private time with God. Eventually, Fosdick regained his spiritual, mental, physical, and emotional health. As a result of what he went through in the insane asylum, Harold Emerson Fosdick wrote a book called *The Meaning of Prayer. It* became a best-selling book. Fosdick argued in The Meaning of Prayer, "I could not have written that book about prayer if I had not gone through that challenging experience." Prayer does change things.

And, at the gravesite of Jesus, Mary Magdalene did what Jesus asked her to do. Jesus told Mary Magdalene, "Go tell my other disciples and Peter that I am alive."

Reverend Jarena Lee and Reverend Maria Stewart did the same thing. They were two (2) outstanding women preachers. They both defend their call to the ministry of Jesus Christ. In their sermon, they preached about what Mary Magdalene did at the gravesite of Jesus. They preached, "Did not Mary Magdalene first preach about the risen Savior, and Is not the doctrine of the resurrection the very first climax of Christianity?" And, they preached, "Did not Mary Magdalene first declare the resurrection of Christ from the dead?"

Oh Yes! Mary Magdalene preached. I can hear her say, "I was there at Calvary when they crucified Jesus upon that old rugged cross. The Roman soldiers tied Jesus' hands and feet to the cross. I saw them drill nails into his hands and feet. I saw them place a crown of thorns on his head. I saw them stick a sword through his side, and Jesus' blood soared to the ground at Golgotha.

I saw on that day that Jesus was crucified that the sun in the sky refused to shine. I noticed that the earth riel and rocked like a drunken man. Oh Yes! Jesus died that Friday night. He was placed in Joseph's borrowed grave, but early Sunday morning, God raised Jesus. That same Jesus is alive today. He lives in my heart, mind, and soul".

Oh Yes! Mary Magdalene is our kind of preacher. She definitely is a powerful preacher. She definitely is a dynamic preacher. She definitely is a spirit-filled preacher. She is definitely a gospel preacher. Oh Yes! Mary Magdalene is definitely our kind of preacher because she preached that Jesus lives.

I serve a risen Saviour, He's in the world today
I know that He is living, whatever men may say
I see His hand of mercy, I hear His voice of cheer
And just the time I need Him He's always near
He lives (He lives), He lives (He lives), Christ Jesus lives today
He walks with me and talks with me
Along life's narrow way
He lives (He lives), He lives (He lives), Salvation to impart
You ask me how I know He lives?
He lives within my heart
In all the world around me I see His loving care
And though my heart grows weary I never will despair
I know that He is leading, through all the stormy blast
The day of His appearing will come at last

He lives (He lives), He lives (He lives), Christ Jesus lives today
He walks with me and talks with me
Along life's narrow way
He lives (He lives), He lives (He lives), Salvation to impart
You ask me how I know He lives?
He lives within my heart.

Mary Magdalene is our kind of preacher. Mary Magdalene is our kind of preacher because she supported the ministry of Jesus. Mary Magdalene is our kind of preacher because she was a conscientious disciple of Jesus. Mary Magdalene is our kind of preacher because she understood the power of the resurrection. Glory Halleluiah! Glory Halleluiah! Glory Halleluiah!

$Acts$ 16:11-15

"A SELLER OF PURPLE"

This morning, I want to preach about the "A Seller of Purple." My subject comes from Acts Chapter 16, verses 11 through 15. I am reading from the New King James translation. I ask you to follow along with me as I read aloud. It reads, "Therefore, sailing from Troas, we ran a straight course to Samothrace, and the next day came to Neapolis, and from there to Philippi, the foremost city of that part of Macedonia, a colony. And we were staying in that city for some days. And on the Sabbath day, we went out of the city to the riverside, where prayer was customarily made, and we sat down and spoke to the women who met there. Now, a certain woman named Lydia heard us. She was a seller of purple from the city of Thyatira, who worshipped God. The Lord opened her heart to heed the things spoken by Paul. And when she and her household were baptized, she begged us, saying, "If you have judged me to be faithful to the Lord, come to my house and stay." So, she persuaded us.

Now, most of us know something about the color purple. Some time ago, Alice Walker wrote a book called

"The Color Purple," which was made into a popular movie. Whoopi Goldberg and Oprah Winfrey were two outstanding actresses in Color Purple. Now, Prince had a song called "Purple Rain." You remember some of the words of that song.

I never meant to cause you any sorrow
I never meant to cause you any pain
I only wanted one time to see you laughing

I never wanted to be your weekend lover
I only wanted to be some kind of friend, hey
Baby, I could never steal you from another

Honey, I know, I know, I know times are changing
It's time we all reach out for something new
That means you, too
You say you want a leader
But you can't seem to make up your mind

Purple rain, purple rain, yeah
Purple rain, purple rain, wooo!
If you know what I'm singing about up here
Come on, raise your hand
Purple rain, purple rain, yeah
I only want to see you
Only want to see you in the purple rain

After the death of my beloved Mother, Elizabeth Murphy-Clayton, I learned that purple was her favorite color. I used to see her wear purple dresses, purple hats, and other purple outfits. But I never asked Momma, Why do you wear purple so often? Isn't that something? Now, on the day of my Momma's homecoming celebration, her children, grandchildren, great-grandchildren, and great-great-grandchildren all wore something purple.

Also, I am a member of the Omega Psi Phi Fraternity Incorporated. Gold and Purple are our fraternity colors. But Do you not know that purple is a sign and symbol of royalty? Yes, it is.

Now, with that in mind, I must put a pin here. I want everyone here to know this. Namely, I do not care how big, tall, or small you are; this is one fact. Now, you may not wear purple, but I want you to know that you are a child of royalty. "You are a chosen people, a royal priesthood, a holy nation, God's special possession, that you may declare the praises of God who called you out of darkness into God's marvelous light" (1 Peter 2). You are a part of a royal priesthood of believers. You are precious in the sight of God. You are a member of the family of royalty. You are a child of God. We know something about purple that the color purple is associated with royalty.

Lydia was a businesswoman. She sold purple fabrics. From all indications, she was also a Single Parent Mother with several children. Therefore, she was either a widower or a divorcee. These are possibilities. Meanwhile, Lydia was originally from Thyritai, another city in Asia Minor. The City of Thyritai was known as a significant city that manufactured and sold purple fabrics worldwide. So, it made sense for my Sisters and my Brothers that Lydia sold purple fabrics.

While she made her money selling purple fabrics, Lydia met Paul at this riverside location in the City of Philippi.

Paul had traveled to the City of Philippi because he had a one-track mind and mission to make Gentiles disciples. He wanted to make disciples and evangelize throughout the world.

Subsequently, Paul meets Lydia at the riverside in the City of Philipp. Here, as a seller of purple, we learned several significant concerns about Lydia. First, **In the first place, Lydia was a seller of purple who believed in the power of prayer.** Indeed, when Paul met Lydia, he learned quickly that she was a businesswoman. That is how she supported herself and her children. But Lydia also she was also a woman who prayed. She was in a prayer meeting with other women when Paul met her. Lydia was there down at the riverside in prayer.

Louise Armstrong was a famous jazz musician and trumpet player from New Orleans, Louisiana. He popularized a song that was part of our African-American History, Heritage, and Culture. Louise Armstrong always performed "Down by the Riverside."

I'm gonna lay down my sword and shield
Down by the riverside
Down by the riverside
Down by the riverside
I'm gonna lay down my sword and shield
Down by the riverside
I'm gonna study, study, war no more

I'm gonna lay down my heavy load
Down by the riverside
Down by the riverside

Down by the riverside
I'm gonna lay down my heavy load
Down by the riverside
Gonna study war no more
I ain't gonna study war no more
Ain't gonna study war no more
I ain't gonna study war no more
Yes, laid down Down by the riverside
Down by the riverside
Down by the riverside

This song, Down by the Riverside, was especially meaningful to our slave fore parents. It was a song about freedom, justice, and equality. This song signaled it was time to get away and leave slavery in the South for freedom in the North. Our slave fore parents ought to have freedom through the underground railroad. So, this is why this song, Down by the Riverside, was so powerful and meaningful to our people. This song was about freedom, justice, and equality for our people and for future generations.

Now, it was at the riverside in the City of Philipp that Paul and Lydia met. When he met her, Lydia was in a prayer meeting. Yes. Lydia believed in the enduring power of prayer. Lydia believed that prayer could change her situation and change her circumstances.

You know, there are different kinds of prayers. First, there is the prayer of interior relaxation and serenity. This kind of prayer does not beg God for anything but in which the soul rests back on God. To be sure, if we are to rest back successfully, we must have something to reset upon like the Psalmist who said, "The eternal God is thy refuge, and underneath are the everlasting arms." We can rest always in God.

Second, there is the prayer of affirmation. This prayer also does not beg God for anything but goes up before the face of God, and there remembers and affirms the great convictions that blow the trumpet in the soul and rouse its powers to action. "The Lord is my shepherd; I shall not want- this is a prayer. Our Father who art in heaven, Hallowed be thy name—this is the prayer of affirmation.

In the third place, there is the prayer of spiritual companionship. This prayer does not beg God for anything but habitually enters into inward fellowship with God. The prayer says with Jesus, "I am not alone because the Father is with me. This is the prayer of spiritual companionship.

Then, finally, we have the prayer of thanksgiving. We are approaching the Thanksgiving Holiday Season. But, in reality, every day for us as a people is always a day of thanksgiving. God has brought us a mighty long way. We must give God thanks for the generations which have preceded us. We must pray daily and thank God for our parents and our ancestors. They sacrifice so much that we would live a better life for future generations, ourselves, and our grandchildren. There is the prayer of thanksgiving.

Now, Lydia sold purple garments and purple fabrics. She was in business to support herself and her children. But, regardless of what you say, Lydia was a woman who believed in the power of prayer. And right now. That was when Lydia met Paul in their prayer meeting. Lydia prayed a prayer of thanksgiving. Can you hear Lydia praying?

"Thank you, Lord. Thank you, Lord. Thank you, Lord. Thank you, Jesus. God, you have brought me a mighty,

mighty, mighty long way. You brought me through sickness and disease. You brought me through when I could not see my way. Glory, Glory, Glory, Halleluiah. God, you brought me a mighty, mighty, mighty long way. Thank you, Lord."

Next, **Lydia, a purple seller, also enjoyed hearing powerful preaching.** She heard some powerful preaching at the riverside in the City of Philippi.

Lydia knew and understood that Paul had something to preach about. Paul had gone through some brutal and terrible life experiences. Paul had been shipwrecked more than once in Jesus Christ's cause and spent a night and a day in the deep. Three times, he said, he received lashed, thirty-nine lashes. Once, he was stoned at Lystra and turned up preaching the next day at Debre, thirty miles away. And he says, I count not myself to have reached my goal. Paul kept on preaching.

Paul had something to preach to Lydia about because Paul had gone through some tough times. Dr. Gardner C. Taylor and the Book of Job also say that tough times help the preacher to have something to preach about.

One night in Dallas, Texas, Dr. Gardner C. Taylor was preaching. His audience was primarily an audience of young preachers. He stated, "The blood marks in the hand are the seal of authority. Now, you may tickle people's fancy, but you will never preach to their hearts until some solemn appointment has fallen upon your own life at some place, and you have wept bitter tears and gone through your won Gethsemane and climbed your won Calvary. That's where power is! It is not in the tone of the voice; it is not in the eloquence of the preacher; it is not in the gracefulness of his gestures; it is not in the magnificence of his congregation;

it is in the heart broken and put together again by the eternal God.

Now, also, The Book of Job believes that when the preacher experiences a difficult time, tough times help the preacher to become more effective. Job says to every preacher,

"God hath fenced up my way that I cannot pass, and he hath set darkness in my paths. God hath stripped me, stripped me of my glory. God had taken the crown off my head. God hath destroyed me on every side. And my hope, God removed it like a tree. God hath kindled his wrath against me. And God hath counted me unto him as one of his enemies. God's troops come together, raise their way against me, and encamp around my tabernacle. God hath put my brethren far from me, and my acquaintances are estranged from me. My kinfolk have failed, and my familiar friends have forgotten me. They who dwell in my house count me for a stranger; I am an alien in their sight. I called my servant, and he gave me no answer. My breath is strange to my wife. Young children despise me; I arose and they spake against me. All my inward friends have abhorred me. My bones cleaveth to my skin and to my flesh" (Job Chapter 19:8-20).

Oh Yes! I advise every preacher and every Christian to read the Book of Job. I advise every preacher to study and learn from older preachers. I advise every preacher to study the teaching and preaching of Paul. Like Dr. Taylor, and Job, Paul was a powerful preacher he live through some tough times.

Paul is a preacher who has gone through some tough, terrible, and trying experiences. But it was through God's grace and God's mercy Lydia heard the powerful preaching of Paul. When Lydia heard the powerful preaching of Paul, I heard Lydia say, "Thank God, I am saved. Thank God, I am saved. I have been brought with a price. Through Jesus Christ, God has washed my sins away and made me whole. Glory Halleluiah, I am saved.

I can hear someone else say, "My hope is built on nothing less Than Jesus' blood and righteousness; I dare not trust the sweetest frame, But wholly lean on Jesus's name, When darkness veils, His lovely face, I rest on His unchanging grace: In every high and stormy-y gale, My anchor holds with within the vale. On Christ, on Christ, On Christ, the solid rock I stand all other ground is sinking sand."

Lydia, as a seller of purple, saw the need to organize a church house. Lydia had a house church. Do you have a house church in your house? Do you have a church in your house? Do you have prayer, singing gospel songs, singing spiritual songs, reading the scriptures, teaching, and preaching in your house? Do you have a church in your house?

Lydia had a church in her house. Lydia's church house included (1) guidelines for a constructive church and (2) guidelines for family religion.

Remember! Paul and Silas were unfairly beaten, arrested, and incarnated in a jail cell within the City of Philippi. They suffered police brutality. Do you know anything about police brutality? Well, talk to the family of George Floyd, other Black families, and people of color here in America.

They will tell you some horrible and personal experiences about police brutality.

But, when Paul and Silas were released from the Philippian jail, they went directly to Lydia's church house. Lydia ministered to Paul and Silas. Lydia provided them shelter, food, clothes, and whatever spiritual support. Lydia possessed a powerful outreach ministry.

And, if this church or any other church is to grow, strive, and survive, it must have a vital outreach ministry. Did you hear what I said? Jesus says, "Go ye therefore to all nations baptizing them in the name of the Father, Son, and Holy Ghost and Lo I will be with you always" (Matthew 28:19-20).

Dr. Jeremiah Wright Jr became the Pastor of Trinity United Church of Christ in Chicago, Illinois. He served there for nearly forty (40) years. President Barack Obama accepted Christ at this church. President Obama and his wife Melissa were married at this church. President Obama and his wife Melissa's two (2) daughters confessed their faith and hope in Jesus Christ, and they were baptized in this church.

But, Pastor Jeremiah Wright Jr grew up in the Grace Baptist Church in Philadelphia, Pennsylvania. His father, Reverend Jeremiah Wright Sr, served as Senior Pastor for over fifty years.

When Pastor Jeremiah Wright Jr became the Pastor of the Trinity United Church of Christ, he and other church leaders came together. Together, they developed some guidelines for a vital outreach ministry. They developed an outreach ministry for future generations to emulate and to carry forward.

The Trinity United Church of Christ has a church planning retreat with all Church leaders. At this retreat, they had a strategy session, a brainstorming session, and a prayer meeting session. This retreat focused on what kind of Church they wanted to leave future generations, their children, and their grandchildren; as a result of this church retreat, Pastor Wright and the Trinity United Christ of Christ accomplished some great things.

The Trinity United Church of Christ grew by leaps and bounds. It grew from 250 church members to more than 11,000 church members. The Trinity Church United Christ learned from Lydia because they did what Lydia did. The Trinity Church developed a vital outreach ministry to reach other believers and non-believers outside the church for the cause of Christ.

And, besides an outreach ministry, Lydia's church house focused on family religion. Family religion was not for Lydia. Instead, the family religion was for Lydia's children. Yes! Lydia made her living selling purple fabric to financially support herself and her children. However, Lydia wanted her children to receive religious instructions. Train up children while they are young; when they become old, they will not depart from it (Proverbs 22:6). Our children must catch religion rather than learn religion. But, they catch religion by watching how Momma, Daddy, Grand Momma, Grand Papa, Auntie, and Uncles live their faith.

Lydia knew that her children were gifts from God and that all children are our future. Children are our most important resource that God has blessed us to have. Will you listen to Whitney Houston? Whitney Houston was a famous rhythm and blues and gospel singer. But, Whitney Houston was raised in the church.

And this is why Whitney Houston's song, "I Believe that the children are our future. Teach them well and let them lead the way. Show them the beauty they possess inside. Give them a sense of pride to make it easier. Let the children's laughter remind us of how we used to be".

Oh Yes! Lydia knew that her children represented a brighter future. Lydia sold purple fabrics to support herself and support her children financially. Oh Yes! Lydia believed in the power of prayer. Lydia enjoyed powerful preaching. Lydia organized a church in her house. God bless you.

$Acts$ 18:18 - 28

OVERCOMING OBSTACLES

I want to preach this morning about "Overcoming Obstacles." My subject grows out of Acts Chapter 18: verses 18-28. I am reading from the New King James translation of scripture. This reads, "So Paul remained a good while. Then he took leave of the brethren and sailed for Syria, and Priscilla and Aquila were with him. He had his hair cut off a Cenchrea, for he had taken a vow. And he came to Ephesus and left them there, but he entered the synagogue and reasoned with the Jews. When asked him to say a longer time with them, he did not consent but took leave of them, saying, "I must by all means keep this coming feast in Jerusalem," but I will return to you, God willing, And he sailed from Ephesus. And when he had landed at Caesarea and gone up and greeted the church, he went down to Antioch. After he had spent some time there, he departed and sent over the region of Galatia and Pyrygia in order strengthening all the disciples. Now a certain Jew named Apollos, born at Alexandria, an eloquent man and mighty in the Scriptures, came to Ephesus. This man had been instructed in the way of the Lord; and being fervent in spirit, he spoke and taught accurately the things of the Lord, though he knew only the baptism of John. So he began to speak boldly in the synagogue. When Aquila and Priscilla heard him, they took him aside and explained to him the way of God more accurately. And when he desired to cross to Achaia, the brethren wrote, exhorting the disciples to receive him; and when he arrived, he greatly helped those who had believed through grace; for he vigorously refuted the Jews publicly, showing from the Scriptures that Jesus is the Christ".

Oprah Winfrey was born in the State of Mississippi to a single-parent mother, and they lived there in abject poverty. Tragically, during this period of her childhood, Oprah was raped and sexually abused by a relative and her mother's abusive boyfriend. This clearly demonstrates that during her early childhood years, she was socially and psychologically traumatized. However, Oprah was sent to Nashville to live with other relatives, where she was able to complete and graduate high school. Oprah eventually made it to Tennessee State University and got a job employed with the media, and, in the process, she became a media broadcaster. Oprah's job as a media broadcaster allowed her to become a national and international celebrity. Now, she has become a billionaire, and Oprah Winfrey has made enough money she will never spend. So, Oprah now uses her wealth to help people in America and throughout the world. Oprah Winfrey is a living witness of someone who has overcome tremendous obstacles.

Now, someone here knows something about overcoming obstacles. You were not supposed to be where you are today.

Somebody or someone here has been told that you were not going to amount to anything, but somehow and someway, by the grace and mercy of God, you are here. You have overcome obstacles.

Now, let me share something about a woman named Priscila. She was married to a man named Aquila. But, although they were wife and husband, Claudia, the Roman Emperor, did not like Christians; in fact, he persecuted Christians in the City of Rome. Claudia persecuted and tragically killed Christians. Therefore, Priscila and Aquila left Rome and subsequently met Paul in the City of Corinth. Priscila and Aquila had much in common with Paul. They were both tenth-makers and committed Christians. They were committed to making disciples for the cause of Christ.

Let me share something about Priscilla. This is because Priscilla overcame obstacles in several manners. **Note that Priscilla demonstrated that she had a positive-minded set**. This evil and despicable Roman Emperor, Claudius, ran her and her husband, Aquila, out of the City of Rome. The City of Rome was known throughout the world.

But Priscilla did not allow the theatrics of Claudius nor the devilish ways of Claudius' to stop her in her tracks. Priscilla and Aquila met Paul in the City of Corinth and began to help him make disciples. Listen! My Sisters and my Brothers, Priscila, had the power to see it through. She was unwilling to let anything in heaven or hell get her way. Priscilla had the power to see it through.

Do you have the power to see it through? I know you are all going through challenging times. But Do you have the power to see it through?

There is one character in the New Testament, mentioned only thrice, concerning whom one suspects many Christians have not heard. His name and some of us are much more like him than the great New Testament figures we know so well. First, in Paul's letter to Philemon, we read, "Demas, Luke, my fellow-workers. So, Demas, along with Luke and named first, was standing by Paul in his Roman imprisonment, a devoted and promising disciple. Second, in Paul's Letter to the Colossians, we read, "Luke, the beloved physician, and Demas." Reading that, one wonders why Demas and Luke, who were praised together at first, were separated in this passage as though Luke indeed retained Paul's confidence as the beloved physician, but Demas had become merely Demas." Third, in the Second letter to Timothy, incorporating, we suppose, one of the last messages Paul ever wrote, we read, "Demas forsook me having loved this present age". Three points on a curve enable us to plot its graph! For here is the story of a man who made a fine beginning and a poor ending: Demas, my fellow worker; Demas, Demas forsook me.

Apostle Paul noted that Demas forsook him. Paul needed Demas's help in the cause of Christ. But Demas forsook him. But Paul did not stop. He kept on moving. Paul had the power to see it through. But Do you have the power to see it through?

Not too long ago, I attended the homegoing celebration of a former church member, Deacon Peter McKisick Jr. He was one of fourteen siblings who grew up in a farming community of Goodwin, Arkansas. Then, he married his devoted wife, Naomi, and they had nine children together. And they raised their children in this same farming community. Deacon Peter McKisick Jr was one of my most faithful, dedicated, and spirit-filled Deacons.

Deacon Barbara McKisick-Haynes is one of Deacon Peter McKissick's younger sisters. At his funeral, she made remarks about him as a family member. She stated, "My brother Peter was twice my Brother. He was both my biological brother and my brother in Christ". I must admit that her remarks about Deacon Peter McKisick, Jr. could have easily been the eulogy. Indeed, Deacon Barbara McKisck-Haynes's remarks were extremely timely and extremely powerful. Her remarks were highly emotional and heartfelt.

Like Priscila, she had the power to see it through. She demonstrated that she knew how to overcome obstacles. Priscila had the power to see through it because she had a powerful mindset. Do you possess a powerful mindset?

Priscila overcame obstacles because she demonstrated that she cared for others. Some people do not care for anyone except themselves. They can all that they can. Then, they set on their can. These are the kind of people who are simply selfish to the core. They are only concerned about me, myself, and I.

But Priscila was not selfish. Instead, she cared for other people. We can see this in how she treats Paul and Apollos. Listen to Paul's words: "Priscilla and Aquilla risk their necks to save me (Romans 16:3). because of that, they will always be my friend. I will always be indebted to Priscilla and her devoted husband, Aquilla."

Now, look at what Priscila did to help Apollos. Apollos was this highly trained and highly educated Christian from Alexandria. He had been trained in rhetoric, Latin, Greek, and persuasion. Apollos was, to some believers, a better preacher than Paul. However, Apollos had an Achilles heel. He knew more about John the Baptist than he knew about Jesus.

I am sad to say this is still the case today. We have some people who know more about John the Baptist than Jesus. And some of these people are Pastors. There is a certain Pastor of a large church in the State of George. He stated that Jesus was 85 percent wrong about most things. And this same Pastor sounds more like Jim Jones every day. This same Pastor tells his members need to grow marijuana, smoke marijuana, and smell like marijuana every day. This Pastor and his congregation need our prayers and help.

But to help this Pastor, I believe he needs to listen to Priscila. Priscila is the woman who knows what she is talking about. Priscilla knew Jesus because she had a personal relationship with Jesus. So, Priscila was elected and selected to teach Apollos something about Jesus.

Someone may ask, "Why did Aquilla not teach Apollos about Jesus?" Well, they were both Christians. But Priscilla was a Roman Christian citizen. She was also born into a wealthy Italian family with money, power, and prestige. Furthermore, Priscilla was better trained and educated than Aquilla in Hellenized culture and philosophy.

Now, please allow me to shout, Brother Aquilla. Typically, and historically, women, for the most part, marry men who have money, power, and prestige. Some single women make it a point to identify men who have money or have the potential to make some money.

Of course, if you do not believe me, I double dare you to attend any college football or college basketball game. And you will see many women hanging around these athletes. I cannot blame them. They want to select and marry someone who can provide her with a better quality of life for herself and any children she will have.

Patrick Mahomes is an African American. His devoted wife is a European American. Now, if you have a problem with interracial marriage, I ask you to quickly get over it. One of these days, your son or daughter may bring someone to dinner. The person your son or daughter may bring to family dinner may be of a different ethnic persuasion. So, I ask you to get ready, get ready.

And, we must understand, And God has made from one [a]blood every nation of men to dwell on all the face of the earth, and has determined their reappointed times and the boundaries of their dwellings, [27] so that they should seek the Lord, in the hope that they might grope for God and find God, though God is not far from each one of us; [28] for in God we live and move and have our being, as also some of your poets have said, 'For we are also God offspring (Acts 17: 26-28)'

Patrick Mahomes is a famous professional football player and Kanas City Chief Professional Football Team quarterback. But he met his wife and the mother of their children when he was a star athlete at Texas Tech University—their meeting and coming together as a couple was more intentional and not necessarily providential. Again, Patrick Mahomes met his future wife in high school and later married. It was the same year that the Kansas City Chiefs won the Super Bowl. Patrick Mahome's wife undoubtedly knew the kind of man that she prayed about needed to marry.

So, I applauded any woman for marrying a man with money. I also applauded any man like Aquila equally. He married Priscilla. Priscilla was a beautiful and intelligent woman, and she was a believer in Christ. Priscilla was also raised in a family with wealth.

So, let me ask this question. Are there any Single Women here like Priscilla? Now, here is what is most important, namely. Priscila overcame obstacles. Although she possessed material wealth, Priscila was more concerned about others than herself. She used her money to help others. Priscilla was philanthropic to the core. She always did what she did to help others.

And Can you hear Priscilla singing?

If I can help somebody as I travel along
If I can help somebody, with a word or song
If I can help somebody, from doing wrong
Then, my living shall not be in vain
Then, my living shall not be in vain
Then, my living shall not be in vain
If I can help somebody, as I'm singing the song
You know, my living shall not be in vain

Also, Priscila overcame obstacles because she knew that she was not alone. Priscila knew that she needed to be a Christian despite everything that was going. Claudius has run her and her husband out of the City of Rome. The City of Rome was known throughout the world.

But, in spite of being run out of Rome, Priscila did not let Claudius stop her. She convinced her husband, Aquilla, that they must always keep first things first. Oh Yes. They were tentmakers. However, they were on a serious mission for the cause of Christ. Priscila and Aquila were Christians with a robust outreach ministry. They used their skill as tentmakers to reach people for the cause of Christ.

Now, please allow me to ask this one question. Can you tell me? Can you advise me? What kind of outreach ministry does this church have? Or What kind of outreach ministry do you have to reach others for the cause of Christ?

Now, Claudius, the Roman Emperor, was evil and sinful. He did everything that he could to frighten and terrify people. He forced Priscila, Aquilla, and other Christians to leave the City of Rome.

But regardless of whatever Claudius did, Priscila was not afraid. Priscilla knew and understood that she was not alone. Priscila had a powerful interior resource. Almighty God was Priscila's interior resource. God was on her side because Priscilla knew from personal experience that the Psalmist was correct. The Psalmist speaks about this across the centuries,

O Lord, You have searched me and known *me*.
You know my sitting down and my rising up;
You understand my thought afar off.
You [a]comprehend my path and my lying down,
And are acquainted with all my ways.
For *there is* not a word on my tongue,
But behold, O Lord, You know it altogether.
You have [b]hedged me behind and before,
And laid Your hand upon me.
Such knowledge *is* too wonderful for me;
It is high, I cannot *attain* it.

Where can I go from Your Spirit?
Or where can I flee from Your presence?
If I ascend into heaven, You *are* there;
If I make my bed in [c]hell, behold, You *are there.*
If I take the wings of the morning,
And dwell in the uttermost parts of the sea,
Even there, Your hand shall lead me,
And Your right hand shall hold me.
If I say, "Surely the darkness shall [d]fall on me,"
Even the night shall be light about me;
Indeed, the darkness [e]shall not hide from You,
But the night shines as the day;
The darkness and the light *are* both alike *to You.*

Oh Yes! Priscilla overcame obstacles. Priscilla had a positive mindset. Priscila cared for other people. Priscila knew she was not alone. Priscilla had God as her interior resource. God will never leave us. God will never forsake us. Never alone. Never alone. No! No! Never alone!

I've seen the lightning flashing And heard the thunder roll, I felt sin breakers dashing, Trying to conquer my soul, God promised never to leave me, No, never to leave me alone; No, never alone. God promised never to leave me- never to leave me alone.

Printed in the United States
by Baker & Taylor Publisher Services